"I have enjoyed your weekly insights for many reasons. Besides being interesting, they are thought provoking, healing, and prompt me to reflect on my life within this world we live in." – Susan Barker

"Thanks for this great blog. You inspired me to write this to my family. We can't all be together this Thanksgiving, and I was feeling sorry for myself. But you made me think about the things that I do have that make me thankful, and that changed everything." – W.M.

"I am thoroughly enjoying your writing series. So informative. It's wonderful to be reminded of essential important things that truly make a difference in our interactions with others and how we connect to our personal day-to-day thoughts and beliefs." – Sofia Costantini

"Thanks again for another great read. I really resonated with your second conclusion about incomplete tasks consuming energy!" – Jillian Best

"I want to tell you what a great job you're doing in writing your Human Capital blog. I really appreciate your work because in my opinion, it is not only very insightful, it's concise, contains a personal anecdote and reveals a great deal of your fine character."-Karen M.

MORE GREAT,
LESS GRIND

Insights to experiencing a better return on our human capital.

PUBLISHING

Library of Congress Cataloging-in-Publication Data
Scott, John

More Great Less Grind\John Scott
1.Non Fiction Mental Health -2. Non-Fiction-Self-Help-Motivation & Inspiration
ISBN: 978-1-990461-14-9 BOOK
ISBN: 978-1-990461-15-6 E-BOOK

1st Printing: December 2021. Printed in Canada

Publisher's Note & Author DISCLAIMER

This publication is designed to provide accurate and authoritative information
concerning the subject matter covered. It is sold to understand that the publisher and
author are not engaging in or rendering any psychological, medical, or other
professional services. If expert assistance or counselling is needed, seek the services
of a competent medical professional. For immediate support, call your local crisis line.
BE WELL

Insight List

1. It's Ok to Close Your Eyes
2. Breathe Like Your Life Depends on It
3. Neuroplasticity in a "Nutshell"
4. Life is Better if First Thing is For You
5. Rest
6. Fuel
7. Movement
8. Mindset
9. Review
10. Listening. It Was Just a Game. Or Was It?
11. Gratitude
12. Mindfulness Part One
13. Mindfulness Part Two
14. Noticing
15. Acceptance
16. Resist Not
17. Choice
18. enVision
19. enRich
20. enJoy
21. Appreciation
22. Flow
23. Awe as an Antidote
24. Pay Attention to the Body-Mind Connection
25. Manwell
26. Sometimes the Energy is Unavailable
27. Truth Zone
28. All That Rushing Didn't Get Me Anywhere
29. Human Capital

DEDICATION

This book is dedicated to my dad for being there. For signing me up for swimming. For the book, The Magic of Believing. For hanging in there for the Games in February, 1997. For the imperfections. For the love.

My dad told me once he wanted to write a book. Then he died too early at age 72. It's always too soon.

Thank you for everything. These 72 Insights are for you.

FORWARD

It seems untraditional for the author to write a foreword for their book, but I wanted to provide context to my mom's comments noted below, when I asked her to do it.

My mom was born on September 10th, 1927. At the time of writing, she is 94. She lives on her own in a very comfortable condo, a big move from the house we six (plus at least one Collie at any given time) lived in as a family.

Her favourite place to be in the world is at her cottage at the beach in Southampton, Canada looking out to Lake Huron. She will swim on calm days and isn't shy to ask someone for help if she needs it to get out of the water.

Her husband, my dad, died in 1997. She misses him every day. And yet, she goes on. She was the eldest of three and survived her brother and sister, who she loved dearly. And yet, she goes on.

A few years ago, her family doctor suggested she get a walker for stability. She gave him "what for" to suggest such a thing. However, recently she has been using a colourful umbrella to provide herself with a little more confidence in walking places—no cane or walker in sight.
When she was 85, I asked her what she wanted to do before she couldn't. She said she had always

wanted to go dog-sledding in the Arctic. So after confirming what I thought I heard, I organized a trip to Inuvik, Northwest Territories, and offered up the idea to my siblings. The look on her face as I took her picture from the tarmac as she paused briefly at the top of the aircraft steps was magical.

With our guide from Arctic Chalet and in about minus 30 degrees Celsius weather, we headed off on four dog sleds to a remote cabin 2 hours away. When we returned, we drove up the frozen Mackenzie River to Tuktoyaktuk on the Beaufort Sea. In Tuk, if you had killed a Caribou or caught a lot of fish, there would be no room in your standard freezer.

So in the 1960s, the community dug an icehouse about 9 metres (30 feet) deep in the permafrost. Although the only way down was a frozen wooden ladder, my mom was up for it or in this case down for it and didn't hesitate to start a careful descent.

Being up for anything is a fair way to summarize my mom's mindset about life. Sure, she has had painful things in her life, like all of us. Once I was driving us through the cemetery on the way out after visiting my dad.

She was sad, and I could see a few tears. Coming down a small hill and turning into a large open area of the cemetery, her sadness morphed into a shared sense of compassion for all the other people who miss their loved ones. It was like she was offering comfort to all those living with memories of dear deceased friends and family. I found her shift from "me" centred to "other" centred to be graceful, natural, and heartfelt.

She is always seeking more understanding by being curious and always seeking more relationships by her social drive.

A few years ago, I took her to the Cancer Centre at a prominent Toronto Hospital to check out the melanoma on her nose. Big waiting room. Deathly quiet. It was easy to feel the strain and stress of people and loved ones about to get an update on their situation.

My mom walks in like this is a great social opportunity. Within a short time, she finds a kindness target, an older man sitting by himself. She gets up from her seat and heads over to say hello, and begins a conversation. I hear her ask about his family, and soon they are both smiling and sharing stories. Somehow it seemed that connection and conversation made the room a little lighter.

When I asked my mom to contribute to the Foreword, she preferred to provide tips on her mindset that she embodies as a "formula" for a long life lived well. Her comments so far at age 94 are:

- Stay curious.
- Be able to laugh at oneself.
- Learn to listen to others.
- Be interested in living life and do it as well as you can.
- Always be grateful.
- Keep smiling.
- Cheezies and Smarties once in a while are just fine

INTRODUCTION

Why More Great, Less Grind?

Feeling great more often is way better than living in the grind for too long.

Several years ago, I was deep in the grind of things, developed two nasty health issues, and wasn't happy as often as I should have been. Then, one day I woke up from denying the stress of it all and thought, "there must be a different way to do my life than that; there must be a better way."

The battery image on this book's front cover represents energy. We know a battery can get drained and depleted, and if that battery is in a flashlight, for example, there just won't be the brightness we need. But conversely, a battery fully charged will provide the power to see and move forward in a better way.

For a few years before beginning to write these Insights, I had a growing feeling that there was something I wanted to say. But I held myself back for a while by paying more attention to thoughts of risk and fear than the inner voice wanting to speak out. Living a busy life that felt like a grind and not handled well, I lost myself in the number of other priorities I set. I had big aspirations for different areas of my life that I thought would be met by long hours and constant effort, the growing stress being something to endure quietly. That didn't work. The grind made me sick.

I didn't label it as burnout, but that's what it was. In 2019, the World Health Organization (WHO) included burnout in their International Classification of Diseases as an occupational phenomenon. WHO defines burnout as follows: "Burnout is a syndrome conceptualized as resulting from chronic workplace stress that has not been successfully managed. Three dimensions characterize it:
1. feelings of energy depletion or exhaustion;
2. increased mental distance from one's job, or feelings of negativism or cynicism related to one's job; and
3. reduced professional efficacy.

Good learning: I know no way to get to where I want to be from constant grind and depletion.

When I was 15, I visited my mother's cousin Bill, a Jesuit Priest who taught at a boy's private school in India. One day, Bill took me to meet Tenzing Norgay, who summited Mount Everest with Edmund Hillary. I recall him being a small man who had a large presence that left me no doubt he was capable of great mental and physical strength. A few years later, I had the luck to meet Edmund Hilary a few times. Although a tall man, he had an equally impressive presence.

These two men fully optimized their skill, intuition, physical and mental strength to do something no person had ever done before. They brought "it" all up the mountain and used all they had to stand on the summit together. Their climb is a great metaphor that exemplifies the potential we all have to ascend to our highest aspirations.

In my teens, I swam competitively. I worked hard, swam with some great swimmers, and had some great coaches. The most memorable race I had was the most effortless swim of my career. Only later, when I understood some of the science of a flow state, did I realize that's what I had experienced. That swim was a personal best and magical race that got me on a Canadian National Team to go to a big international meet in New Zealand, which was a big deal for me. At the busiest part of my swimming career, I swam 11 workouts a week plus dryland workouts.

Somehow the "formula" of good sleep, enough food, a pretty focused mindset, and effort in my training to handle the workload came easily to me. It seemed pretty simple that if I wanted to swim faster, I had to do certain things, like being healthy and rested, to endure the training.

Later on, I swam across Lake Ontario (51km) twice and part of Georgian Bay ((32kms). I still hold the fastest time in the world across the traditional route of Lake Ontario and am the first person to swim from Christian Island to Collingwood.

Through the swims, I raised money for Children's Wish and Special Olympics. Then I became the youngest Chairman of a Special Olympics World Games that we hosted in Toronto and Collingwood in February 1997. Halfway through the four-year preparation at a tricky spot, I promised myself a reward if we pulled off "the best Games ever" by climbing Mount Kenya and Mount Kilimanjaro afterward.

After all this, work became busier; I married and felt I slowly lost focus on myself and the formula I knew for sustained enjoyment and performance.

Soon I started the slow burnout. And on that day, when I woke up and decided to do my life differently, the first thing I did was create a new journal heading called Magical Moments to focus on what I wanted to experience more of. That one thing made a world of difference.

Then I looked at and made changes to my sleep, diet, exercise, and my mindset. These four domains of life had transformative effects once I adjusted them to serve me better.

When I started working in the financial industry, someone told me that an older colleague who had retired nine months before had just died of a heart attack. A friend younger than me died of a heart attack last year. And recently, three close male friends in my age group have had life-threatening heart issues.

I am very grateful and proud of myself for having stopped the decline in my wellbeing. Once I made the shift, I felt happier more often, my two health issues faded away, and I enjoyed work and was much more productive.

I got let go from my job in a major corporate downsizing, and between jobs, I took courses in mindfulness, positive psychology, emotional intelligence, and compassionate leadership.

I have worked in good cultures and not so good ones. I've experienced leadership done well and not so well. I teared up reading the first part of the book," Dying for a Paycheck," by Jeffrey Pfeffer, about how corporations hurt people.

This partial list of observations and experiences created a growing interest in how we do life and, ideally, sustain a healthy level of wellbeing. I am fascinated by optimizing our unique resources to climb the "mountain" we aspire to. In the grind, there is contraction, like survival mode, not much room for joy and fulfillment, but there is expansion when we are experiencing the great in life.

Growth is a natural state. We know this from the real-time feedback system of our bodies: a good night's sleep, after a day of exercise, healthy food, and a clear mind support thriving, and we can feel that like all things are possible.

I love this quote by Roger Banister, "I knew I had a sub-four-minute inside me, somewhere." Of course, this is optimal performance, but my meaning isn't that we have to climb mountains, swim large bodies of water or run super fast.

My message is that we all deserve to be happy, healthy, and feel good about our lives. And when we are in that place, we can most fully utilize our unique human capital, becoming a little better from wherever we are.

These Insights are about improving wellbeing. If we make choices that support our wellbeing, if we care for our minds and bodies a little more, we are much more able to see the need and make an effort towards greater global wellbeing.

Grind is no good for anyone; great is better for everyone. There is a better way, and that is why I wrote these Insights.

Insight One:
It's Ok to Close Your Eyes

When you return to flying, you'll be reminded, "In the event of a loss in cabin pressure, secure your oxygen mask before helping your children or others." We've had a severe "loss in cabin pressure" lately, and it is taking an enormous toll economically and in terms of mental health. If we look after ourselves, we can best help our loved ones and others in our circle.

It's ok to close your eyes. It's ok to take a break. To rest is ok. High-performing athletes do this exceptionally well. Our experience of sight requires up to 30% of our brain activity. Closing our eyes provides immediate rest for our brain. And breathing, like our life depends on it, while our eyes are closed, is well, a beautiful thing. Our brains weigh about 3lbs or 2% of a 150lb body and require 25% to 30% of the fuel we consume for roughly 100 billion neurons. Our brain is the master regulator for our whole body (30 to 40 trillion cells).

Our brain needs care. Being on all the time causes stress and depletion. We are washing our hands a lot and yet not practicing brain hygiene as much as we should.

Closing your eyes during the day to take a micro rest, taking a walk, deciding to slow down, and unlearning rushing or eating a healthy meal are examples of self-care. Time for you is ok. You matter. And a break, a walk, a pause doesn't mean you are less of a parent, uncaring for others, or a bad employee.

Many people are pretty good at helping others and not as good at being kind to themselves as a behavioral habit. I asked a dear friend how she was doing the other day, and it brought tears to her eyes to the degree to which she rarely thinks about her caring for herself.

It's hard to argue that generally, men are not skilled at looking after themselves. I often know that a tough exterior intends to reflect we are the best of the best; we are handling it all. "Tough" guys (and gals) don't need the sleep others do and consume lots of beer and wine to ease the stress. We often are privately self-critical. Showing our emotion, expressing feelings, being just as we are might be seen as weak.

This imbalance or misalignment is not a requirement and is unhealthy. Each of us can be an equal priority with others in our lives. Energy consumers are imbalance and misalignment, and energy creators are balance, alignment, humility, authenticity, and compassion. We will live longer and be healthier with the latter.

Designed to thrive, each of us has a birthright to be happy, healthy, and fully alive. Of course, we all want that for our children. It's ok to want to be happy, healthy, and fully alive for ourselves too.

We all experience painful things in life. Our opportunity is to understand that self–compassion, a desire to alleviate the suffering, is available to us and has significant benefits:
- Highly correlated with increased wellbeing, positive emotions, and resilience.
- Reduction in depression, anxiety, and risk of burnout.
- It allows energy for compassion for others and builds stronger relationships.
- Self-compassion is a strength, a Super Power!

Rightly so at this time, there is considerable recognition of and appreciation for frontline workers. Additionally, others in some essential services get that well-deserved recognition and our respect.

Maybe we could all think of ourselves as frontline workers and offering essential services. As parents with kids at home or elderly parents, we can feel the need to be activated to help. In that context, we are frontline workers. We offer an essential service of the support, patience, and attention required to help others through this time. We are critical to many people in our circle or network.

11

For example, people in the financial services sector, the business I have been in, dealing directly or indirectly with people who have lives and are providing love and economic security for their children, are essential frontline workers. Might we consider that we all offer a necessary service to ourselves? Not just at this time but all the time. It is vital to be living a full, productive, and happy life to optimize body and mind. It's hard to be happy when depleted.

- I can't be mentally fit and resilient at "one bar" of power.
- It's hard to express our uniqueness at the highest possible level by not caring for ourselves.
- Hard to see the mind-blowing miracle of evolution from one-celled organisms 3.5 billion years ago to human beings today in a fog of fatigue and self-criticism.

If you are experiencing unhealthy stress and not happy most of the time, there is a different way to do life that can start now. Here are some ideas to get you moving on that better route:
- Breathe deeply, exhale slowly (internal "switch" calms us down).
- Try to get 7 to 9 hours of good sleep.
- Choosing an exercise as simple as a pleasant walk-in nature is excellent for the system.
- Meditation is a sustainable performance habit. Check out Calm.com.

Headspace.com and MUSE, the Headband.

- Eat well. The only things that fuel you are what you eat and drink.
- Before you fall asleep, review at least three good facts from the day.
- Gratitude – be grateful. If this stumps you; remember you are breathing; start there!
- Be kind – to yourself and others. We have little information about how others are coping these days—tilt on the side of compassion and kindness.

May you be well. It's better that way.

Insight Two:
Breathe like Your Life Depends on It

On June 28th, 2010, I turned on my phone, clicked on the Evernote app, and sat down to make notes in my journal. The journal captured many of the day-to-day challenges, frustrations, irritants, and general tough stuff that I felt were in my life. At that time, I had two nasty healthy issues evolving and was exhausted. I sat there staring at the Evernote app, that little vertical cursor line flashing, waiting for me to start typing, like a tapping foot. As I was about to start typing, I thought that this couldn't be right. There must be a different way to do life than this.

I had been trying to be the best husband, best Dad, the best son to my mom, and the best Branch Manager I could, "wiring" that I see now was somewhat faulty: certainly not sustainable. So, still looking at my Evernote app, I decided to start a new journal heading called Magical Moments and began to write most days about anything I noticed that was magical and made me happy.

My first entry was, "Sunday night putting Taylor to bed. She wasn't moving quickly, and I stayed calm (cause for recognition here, just on that point!). She got her clothes ready for Monday and some gifts for her kindergarten teacher (end of school). Finally, teeth brushed, she picked three books to read, her "favourites," and we read them, snuggled up closely. Kisses and hugs, partly playing and reading. Great, really great."

Choosing to hold back and take a new perspective was a pivotal and trajectory-changing moment for me, feeling like I went from a mindset of madness to magical. That act of self - something, care, love, survival also moved me to look into my sleep, which was a mess and a diet lacking in protein after seeing a nutritionist. Both I fixed quickly. More energy and aliveness replaced exhaustion.

One of those stress-induced nasty health issues was an increasing frequency and severity of migraines. Disclaimer: I'm not a doctor. Seek your medical advice. My GP sent me to see a specialist at St. Mike's Hospital, who said, "Yup, you have migraines with aura," and you can take some drugs that might help. Not satisfied, a friend suggested going to a naturopath. He gave me magnesium glycinate and vitamin B complex, which quickly reduced the migraines to rare, mild events. On the way out, he called after me and asked, "by the way, how do you breathe?' I stopped at the door, looked back, and asked, "What?"

That question and discussion led to learning to breathe better and the regular practice of meditation. Right now, try taking a few deep breaths. First, breathe, so you know you're breathing. Feel the air pulled in through your nose, and feel your lungs expanding. Notice the slight pause as your breathing transitions to an exhale. Then feel your lungs releasing, and the air flowing back out through your nose and notice the transition to another inhale.

On average, a person at rest takes about 16 breaths per minute, 960 breaths/hour, 23,040 breaths/day, 8,409,600 a year, and so on until the last exhale. Breathing is life. Breathing in triggers our sympathetic (activation), and breathing out triggers our parasympathetic (relaxation response) nervous systems. A longer inhale than exhale activates the body, and a longer exhale than inhale relaxes the body. An even count on inhales and exhales promotes a balanced, focused feeling.

To get activated quickly, you could breathe into the count of 6 and exhale to 4. To relax and get calmer, you could inhale to the count of 4 and exhale to 6. Various names refer to a technique to promote reduced stress, balance, and a requirement for focus: square breathing, 4 X 4, or as the military and first responders like to call it, tactical breathing. Square breathing entails breathing to the count of 4, holding for 4, exhaling for 4, and holding for 4. Of course, you can adjust these counts to your comfort and ease. Repeating these at least three times will do the trick.

The brain needs our care to be optimal, including a diet (the brain requires up to 30% of our resources), exercise, sleep, and getting skillful at managing our 50,000 to 70,000 thoughts, of which about 70% are negative. Even for 3 to 5 breaths, focusing on breathing will quiet the sometimes storm of thoughts, reduce stress, and trigger our natural relaxation response. These are high-performance strategies that universities are teaching, the military uses, government and athletes use.

I love these comments from a young girl describing deep breathing as a means to reduce stress, "It's kinda like if you had a jar of water and then the jar would be your brain and then you put glitter in the jar and then if you shook up the jar and the glitter went everywhere that would be how your mind works." And she continues, reflecting on the breathing practice she has learned, "It's like all the sparkles are at the bottom of your brain."

Be grateful for every breath! May you be well. It's better that way,

Insight Three:
Neuroplasticity in a "Nutshell"

Our sometimes-nutty brain changes itself throughout our lives by our thoughts, experiences, and environment. USER CAUTION: the good and bad news is that the brain is indifferent: what we think and experience, what we "feed it," will become more pronounced. Our mind directs our brain: good input, good output, bad input, bad output.

William James, a famous American philosopher and psychologist, considered to be the leading thinker of the late 19th century, knew that "The greatest discovery of my generation is that a human being can alter his life by altering his mind's attitudes. As you think, so shall you be."

The term neuroplasticity was first used in 1948 by a Polish scientist. And in 1949, Donald Hebb, a Canadian neuropsychologist, became famous for saying, "neurons that fire together, wire together." However, it wasn't until about thirty years ago that it became widely accepted that the brain changes throughout a lifetime and is not a "fixed" organ after childhood.

In my previous Insight, I spoke about my journaling theme going from madness to magical. In 2010, I woke up to do my life differently: from stress, depletion, and related health issues to an overall healthier physical and mental outlook. As a result, I began to practice being aware of and writing about magical things in my life, in effect, something for which I was grateful.

Within about three weeks, I felt good more often, felt more at ease, and more easily saw and appreciated what was good in my life: an example of neuroplasticity.

Ralph Waldo Emerson said, "You become what you think about all day long."

What we dwell on and experience changes the brain to create thoughts that support those changes. Therefore, since about 70% of our thoughts are negative, we must be careful about which thoughts to believe.

"The greatest weapon against stress is our ability to choose one thought over another." - William James.

I found my thinking (challenges, frustration, and tough stuff) conflicted with my real intention or my inner aspirational voice: what I wanted. Misalignment. Turbulent thinking. I could have ramped up the bad feelings, and it wouldn't have made me happier. Only feeling happier through an altered perspective and dwelling on that made me happier (and healthier).
No amount of feeling bad will make us feel good, and berating oneself for things not completed or not

19

done as skilfully as we would have liked, dishonours that which is good and part of our highest ambition.

Before COVID and self-distancing, I played doubles tennis with my wife and two friends next to a singles game. One guy, who I can only assume was Andy, kept berating himself out loud. "Oh Andy, that was a bad shot," "Andy, WHAT are you doing!", "Andy, you KNOW better!" It felt like a Seinfeld episode: a hostile self-talking tennis player. How could that be enjoyable? Andy seemed to completely ignore his many great shots, let alone the possible perspective of being hugely excited to play at a fantastic club. There was no "Andy, wow, beautiful shot!" "Andy, SWEET serve!" "Andy, that was a perfect shot, and it felt SO good!'

My message to Andy is to consider the good and great shots: learn from others. It matters what we pile into our brains. Your future depends on it. Let go of what doesn't serve us. Practice awareness to bring into alignment our self-talk with our highest ambitions. Focus on what is going on that is good, not what isn't good. Hold the goal in mind, lean in while embracing the good. Use good facts as super fuel.

Once in the car on the way to school, my daughter said, "Oh, dad, I'm sorry. I forgot my assignment. I'm so mad at myself. I'm so upset." I said, "just now, my love, you remembered, the forgetting happened a while ago. You are a very good rememberer. Let's go back and get it!"

Right thoughts, aligned to our authentic and most inspired dreams, change the brain in the right direction and support a more comfortable "ride."

Consider:
- It's ok to take a break, to close your eyes. Suggest sitting quietly, ideally with your eyes closed, and allowing your body to relax and experience doing nothing for three minutes, except breathing.
- To regain balance and calm, try a breathing exercise of an inhale for four, hold for four, exhale for four and hold for four, five times.
- Each evening after the lights are out, review three good facts from the day and why they were good.
- Start a gratitude journal, writing down things for which you are grateful.
- With a big smile, say to someone, "I am so grateful for what you do."

May you be well. It's better that way.

Insight Four:
Life is Better if First Thing is For You

I once pitched a senior leader in a prominent wealth management firm on resilience training with his Advisors. He said emphatically, "We have no resilience problem here!" I gave him an example of an Advisor friend of mine at his firm who told me when talking about stress, "Are you kidding? I'm freaking out before I even get to the office." That stopped this leader for a few seconds but not long enough to know what to do with it.

Goldman Sachs does get it and has had a robust resilience program for almost ten years. They know that taking a broader role in supporting their sales and service people is good business. Sales and service people are like high-performance athletes. I think wealth management leadership has an opportunity to see more clearly there being ROI in supporting sustainable performance. We all know examples of the risks inherent in unsustainable performance.

We have two almond-shaped amygdalae, one in each hemisphere. Small and powerful. Ancient. Two hundred million years of practice at emotional memory and charged responses. That's where fear, anxiety, and aggression are felt and get triggered. Freaking out inside or outside is known as an amygdala hijack. Adrenaline and cortisol are released very fast. Our amygdalae react to imagined threats too. The same area of our brain "lights up," whether a real or an imagined threat. The good news is that with training, we can create a pause before a reactive response. Nice.

Depowering the hijack effect is done by attention training, which coincidentally powers up the prefrontal cortex (self-regulation). We are so crazy cool. The morning is a great time to practice training attention and positively correlates with a good day!

When we wake up, our minds are usually clear, having just had, we hope, a good night's sleep. Part of each day's success is determined by how the previous day ended—plan on getting enough sleep so that you can rise easily in the morning. In addition, it would help to get ahead of the inevitable influx of thoughts that may hijack our day. New habits can take a bit of effort to implement: a comfortable sense of ease is essential. Be easy on yourself if this is a new habit you want to implement.

Rise well. I suggest you plan to get up a little earlier than usual to have the time to practice comfortably.
- Make your bed, unless there's someone still in it! *(Great book! "Make Your Bed: Little Things That Can Change Your Life by William McRaven). F*eels good to start the day with a completion. Completions are energy creators.

- Find a quiet place to sit where you won't be disturbed. Having a regular place helps prime the brain for making this a habit.
- Sit quietly and breathe. Back straight. Feet flat on the floor. Allow your body to become relaxed. You could do a body scan by starting with bringing attention to your feet, relaxing your legs, relaxing your buttocks on the chair, relaxing your torso, and letting your shoulders relax, and just sitting and breathing. Try for 2 or 3 minutes. Build to 5 to 10 minutes.
- Make 2 to 3 intentions for the day: Could be business or personal—completing an essential task for work. Or exercise or to be present or eat a healthy lunch or feel good throughout the day.
- Keep a journal handy to write down insights and reminders. Reviewing goals at least once a week is helpful.
- Either write or dwell on three things for which you are grateful.
- Consider constructing an affirmation or statement or prayer that fully supports you in having the day and life you desire.
- Stand up tall, shoulders back, smile, and carry on with your day with relaxed intention.

I think our job is to do the work that brings us alive. Starting each day, settled and in control, practicing self-direction creates the patterns that support optimizing the route!

24

Think Roger Federer, walking onto centre court. Control. Leaning in with confident anticipation. Ready to take care of business.

May you be well. It's better that way.

Insight Five:
Rest

Start of a four-part series that are foundational to elevated and sustained performance: Rest. Fuel. Movement. Mindset. They all matter.

First up … Rest

Summary: If you're tired, sleep more. That's it.

Giraffes are good to go with about 2 hours of sleep. Brown bats need 20. Humans need 7 to 9 hours a night, then good things happen, like thriving. But we are the only mammal that willingly delays sleep and, right, not so optimal. Studies show that lack of sleep may cause Alzheimer's and linked to other health problems, including:

- Cognitive dysfunction / depression / stress / type II diabetes / weight gain / heart disease.

Your employer should have an interest in how well you sleep too. Or maybe I'm just dreaming.

Proper sleep supports improved immune function and memory, speeds up repairs, and generally optimizes performance. I know we are serious, sales and service people to lots of money, teachers, lawyers, laborers, aspiring leaders, parents to magical kids, great golfers, keen cyclists, aspiring musicians, or a spouse. But, before all that, we are, you are, the most successful and stunningly complex cooperation of ~30 trillion cells in the known universe: it needs sleep to feel good and last.

Your brain is either awake and aware or asleep and cleaning up. Sleep activates a waste removal system: cells shrink, and water is flushed around, taking out gunk (neurotoxins). Brain hygiene is good for thriving. Sleep helps.

I swam competitively as a kid and did some crazy hard workouts. I still hold the world speed record for swimming across the traditional route of Lake Ontario (51km) and have climbed a couple of big mountains.

Fact: Sleep is critical to healthy high performance: training, maintaining fitness, muscle repair and recovery, mindset, goal attainment, and enjoyment. You are a high-performer. Don't get to empty. Sleep isn't a leisure activity; it's a high-performance activity.

After getting married, we had three daughters, and I had growing responsibilities at home and work. Doing for others in every category was my strategy, looking for the "award" for best dad, the best husband, best manager. My sleep quality declined and contributed to a feeling of depletion and health issues. Personal belief: "Tough guy." Evidence above.

Must take care of everyone else first. My ego cared more about holding up all of that "best of" status than it did about the risk to what I wanted: to be happy and healthy. Not attending to healthy sleep was crushing.

I used "Rest" at the outset purposely to broaden the context of recovery. Sleep is the most significant element of rest. I also wanted to link back to the first Insight, "It's ok to close your eyes." The brain loves little micro-breaks or even a short nap. Lots of athletes take naps. Closing your eyes for a minute or two is a great way to quickly restore and reset your focus and create pauses that unlearn rushing.

Practical and instantly available tip:
When moving between meetings or during long projects or to transition between work and family:

- Sit quietly, tall back but not rigid. Close your eyes, breathe deeply, fully into your lungs, and allow your body to relax on each slow, long exhale.
- Face softening, shoulders letting go, following your breath, use some time, even for a minute to rest the "system," smile, breathe deeply, and exhale slowly.
- Open your eyes and proceed to the next call or activity feeling refreshed and present, be where you are in that moment: not still in a past conversation or a future one. Just right now. The other person will love that attunement.

Sleep Prep:
- Not eating within a few hours of sleep time helps.
- Check out any possible sleep disorders like sleep apnea (low or paused breathing – that can't be good!)
- Exercise promotes good sleep.
- No alcohol before sleep.
- Make sleep a priority. Consistent times are healthier.
- Relaxed mind before sleep.
- Avoid blue light from technology.
- And my favourite, just before lights out, dwell for a few minutes on good facts from the day or run through a few things for which you are grateful.

"Get some rest, Pam. You look tired." Jason Bourne

Be kind out there. Things are better that way.

Insight Six:
Fuel

Rest. Fuel. Movement. Mindset ... Matter. I am focusing on each of these sustainable performance elements in a four-week series.

Second course is Fuel.

There are lots of emotions and cultural traditions around food. When I am down and tired, I tend to eat less well. Weak will. More crappy processed food: after, remorse. When I feel rested and have the "all things are possible" mindset and busting with living, I make better food choices. And there are strong cultural traditions related to food like feasting, celebrations, and showing generosity.

We eat together—heaps of food at family gatherings. Eyes go big and wide, wired to eat it all. It's not from our mother who told us to finish our meal because there are starving kids in Africa so much as it is because thousands of years ago, the next mealtime was unknown. Sometimes we use food as a reward or to soothe anxiety. Food is a messy topic.

After my dad died of prostate cancer at 72, I somewhat unconsciously reduced all meat protein types in my diet. That became a problem. Iwas tired a lot and much less resilient—sore muscles. But restoring muscles isn't the only thing for which there is a requirement for protein. Every system in our body needs energy from what we eat. Protein is also vital in keeping our immune system healthy, from our skin to our digestive tract and white blood cells. For example, our bodies regenerate about 300 billion cells a day.

Our skin, the only thing between our inside and outside, replaces itself about every two weeks. And like poor sleep habits, there are significant risks and consequences to a bad diet. For example, consuming too much sugar is associated with heart disease, stroke, obesity, diabetes, high blood cholesterol, cancer, and cavities.

I did a mindful eating exercise a few years ago. The idea is to use a raisin (or maybe a piece of chocolate!). Hold it, Feel it. Smell it. Be curious about where it came from and how it got to be in one's hand. Listen to it as the fingers roll it around. Next, put the raisin in one's mouth and move it around with your tongue. Bite into it gently and sense the juice coming from it. Feel the texture after it has been bitten and masticated, then swallow it.

As I was swallowing the raisin, I had a powerful image come to mind of the back of my throat being like Niagara Falls. And when that raisin dropped off the cliff down into my body, I thought, "Holy crap, everything that goes into my mouth goes over the falls and right into my body! Everything that goes over becomes part of me!"

Awareness is good.

Dan Buettner is an author who has studied five regions around the world where people live exceptionally long lives. Common elements of a blue zone diet are nutrient-dense vegetables, mostly green leafy vegetables, fruits, herbs, nuts, seeds, sweet potatoes, corn, and whole grains. Blue zone inhabitants also eat a lot of legumes and beans. Blue Zones

In 2004 Jamie Oliver introduced healthier lunches to a British school. Within a month, teachers reported students had better attention, improved memory, and overall behaviour. The nurse reported a sharp decline in the medication she was administering and a decline in asthma and other illnesses. In a study at a prison, 1,000 inmates got a regular fish oil supplement. After one year, violent behaviour was down 33%, sociability was up, and they experienced overall health improvement.

Estimates are that 40% of how you feel now is attributable to your last meal.
Lean muscle tissue is 75% water, our brains are 80% water, and blood is 95%. Therefore, for our entire body and mind to operate optimally, we need to be fully hydrated. None of our bodily systems can speak in words, but they do in feelings in the short term and speak loudly in the long term by illness or wellness.

Choices.

There is no question that good food and hydration support physical and mental high, sustainable performance, feeling good, and living long, well. And such great news, the body is super resilient and happy to accept fuel upgrades at any age or stage that make it operate better and last longer.

"Eat food. Not too much. Mostly plants." Michael Pollan, American author, journalist, and activist.

Eat well … mostly. It's better that way,

Insight Seven:
Movement

Four-part series on Rest. Fuel. Movement. Mindset. So, let's roll with Movement.

Summary: When we move, we feel good.

But before moving along, I'd like to say something about gratitude—a good friend of mine when young was a successful model and aspiring to a long career. At 23, she was in a car that a drunk driver hit. She suffered massive internal and external damage. Her chosen vocation was over, and she had to learn to walk again. From then to now, at 68, she has had considerable physical challenges. A few weeks ago, I saw her strolling along a quiet country road in an area where we both have a place. She struggles with a rare problem of her fascia, which encloses and stabilizes muscles, shrinking, making it very painful to walk.

I am so grateful I can move with ease.

Yesterday I drove my 92-year-old mom to her beloved cottage on Lake Huron's shore to spend the summer there. She wanted to talk, and I wanted to finish this Insight. However, I felt ashamed that I was frustrated with her and became non-communicative, so I went for a run.
Observations:

34

- I intended to run and did it well. I got what I call an intention gift: planning to do something and feeling a boost or a gift of amplified experience. Completions are neurologically very positive.
- An idea dropped in for something I wanted to say in this letter. Nice!
- I became aware of distracting thoughts a few times, thinking of yesterday and tomorrow: my body running and my mind somewhere else. Ever have that feeling?
- Bringing my mind back to the present moment, aligning with my body to fulfill the intention, and maximizing the run felt empowering.
- Back at the cottage, I felt a freshness and calm concerning the stress I had felt earlier. I quickly took up a conversation with my mom that lasted through dinner and into the evening—rich shift: endorphins (feeling good) out powering cortisol (feeling stress).

A friend relates this story "I was feeling pretty good that I was out for a run. I had my sensor in my shoes to monitor my planned pace of 5-minute kilometers. I knew my marathon training pace well. I looked at my monitor, and I was doing exactly 225 cm/stride, equating to my goal pace. After a bit, my mind wandered, and I began to reflect that I hadn't run as regularly as I had planned. I started to get down on myself and mad, thinking about why I hadn't run much recently. I then looked at my monitor, and I had slowed to a 200 cm/stride, which equates to 5

1/2-minute kilometers." Then he said to me, "I have empirical evidence that my thoughts were holding me back."

Oddly, when we sit all day, it's exhausting. Studies suggest our ancestors used to walk 12 to 18 kilometers a day. Movement is an energy creator. High-intensity training, short bursts of fast or strenuous exercise are proven to reduce depression. I love high-intensity training because, for me, it lifts my fitness level faster and more sustainably than regular training.

Movement strategies:
- During the workday, stand up at regular intervals to move around.
- Use a Bluetooth headset so you can move around.
- Consider a desk that can shift to a stand-up desk.
- Exercise regularly and allow yourself to feel great about improvements from your level of fitness.
- Walking is an excellent and underrated exercise.
- Attention and intention are powerful ways to stay on track and train personal empowerment.

Pharmaceutical companies offer a collection of drugs they would like us to buy: medicines that can improve our immune system, reduce anxiety and depression, clear up our skin, boost self-confidence, improve our sex life, and a myriad of other ailments, or we can exercise.

Take a walk, or hike or run or cycle or garden, or something. It's better that way!

Insight Eight:
Mindset

Fourth of a four-part series on Rest. Fuel. Movement and Mindset.

A mindset could be like a thermostat. Instead of cold, it says crazy, instead of hot, happy: ideally on happy.

"Hey, who is messing with my mind setting?"

"The mind is its own place, and in itself can make a heaven of hell, a hell of heaven." John Milton, Paradise Lost

In Insight Two, I related that I was in a very unhealthy place for a while and saw lots of things as frustrating and stressful. Instead of seeing all the good clearly, my thoughts were in kind of a hell of fatigue and depletion. I also related waking up from that mindset and shifting to feeling better much more often. Part of that shift was seeing the same things I saw before but differently. That is neuroplasticity or mental relief.

I think one of the most worthwhile personal endeavors is to build awareness. And in this context, awareness of our thoughts. So often, we think about how our life should be, what is missing, or what we haven't accomplished. And stories we tell ourselves of not being good enough, or intelligent enough, or not enough of something or the other.

My 92-year-old mother will refer once in a while to not being clever. When she was little, she had trouble with school and failed a grade. Somehow not being smart stuck. My sister let me know she was frustrated with my mom at the slow pace as they went through a box of old bills. I told her to tell my mom she is bright for taking it so seriously.

I told my mom that her belief doesn't serve her. And that she is mistaken in her opinion because I observe that she often exemplifies intelligence in many of its forms like curiosity, insight, wisdom, and common sense. I felt like I was speaking to a healing child. That felt good for both of us.

We can, through paying attention, build awareness of our thoughts. First, check for evidence of the validity of the thought. What is the origin of the thought? What, then, is the truth?

When we were born, our parents looked at us the same way we looked at our child: immeasurable, unconditional love. We don't have to go through life with less than that for ourselves.

What if the story we tell ourselves isn't true? What if we are mistaken?

Carol Dweck has written about the growth mindset and a fixed mindset. A growth mindset is the mindset of possibilities, learning, openness to personal growth, and expansion. A fixed mindset holds one's traits and values as fixed and not changeable, and anything that shows up disrupting that view is wrong. Like saying all day long that it is everyone else's issue. Not me. The problem is out there.

If that person I have in mind right now could take those thoughts, hold them on a table, and look at them, maybe, he could learn something and grow and suffer less.

When I went through new advisor training, it was often asked, "Who is driving the bus?" Sometimes our minds take over, and before you know it, you aren't driving anymore.

Our minds are busy and evolutionarily designed for distraction and monitoring threats, so they have a natural negativity bias. Remembering bad things or faults sticks like Velcro, and positive traits and successes are like Teflon, sliding off. This negativity bias doesn't serve us much anymore, so we will benefit significantly by being discerning.

Here are some ideas to create your formula to maintain a positive and growth-oriented mindset:
- Proper rest, right fuel, and movement help form a solid ground from which to pay attention.

- Practice becoming aware of thought patterns.
- Ask: Do they serve us? What is the truth?
- Create an affirmation or prayer, or mantra that reflects our reality and inspired mindset.
- Choose to reframe mistakes or "failures" as learning.
- Dwell on positive facts that support our inspired future.
- Stand in our full height, smile, shoulders back, and lean into our positive future.

Don't believe every thought. It's better that way!

Insight Nine:
Review

Review of the last four weekly Insights of Rest, Fuel, Movement, and Mindset.

Summary: Rest, fuel, movement, and mindset matter. Do them well for more life.

For ages, people have considered why we are here. What is our purpose?

Big question.

I think our purpose is to feel a sense of aliveness: to be fully alive. So when we feel alive, being who we are, and doing what we love to do, those are pretty good clues to a more specific purpose or sub-purpose.

Growth is a natural state. In that place, we feel good, and decline doesn't —two significant signals from the body: feeling good or bad.

Practicing awareness is like signing up for mind and body "Alerts."

Wen we thrive, we are on purpose. Our purpose is synonymous with expressing ourselves at the highest possible level, just like any other part of nature.

It's good to have a guidance system, a "why?" or a north star to follow in our life at home and work. Why do we go to work where we work? Why do we do what we do? What is our purpose when we speak to a friend or client? You might say, "I am calling to do some business." Or, "I work here because I need money," "I do what I do because I am good at it."

You can integrate or infuse that job or call with that higher level of purpose: aliveness. How can we be our best at home with our family? How can we bring our best self to work? How can we be our best in each call or interaction in a sustainable way?

When I was preparing to swim across Lake Ontario in 1992, I trained a lot, probably more than anyone who had attempted the 51- kilometer swim. One day I went to my regular outdoor pool to work out. It was a cold and rainy day. The lifeguards were wearing their full-body, warm-up hooded jackets. As I entered the pool deck, one of the lifeguards called to ask, "What are you doing here?" I turned around and asked her to repeat the question. "Well," she said, 'it's cold and rainy, and no one else is here." The best response I could give was to tell her that the weather or the fact no one else was in the pool didn't matter to me. I had a plan to swim across the lake in record time, and if I didn't show up because it was cold or rainy, that would lower the odds of me completing the swim. I had 100%

alignment between my purpose and my actions, so much so that I couldn't understand her question.

While that story is true, it isn't really about training to swim across a lake. It's about aligning action with something that brings you alive. If you don't run and aspire to run a 3km and do it, or even try, that is cause for celebration. If you're overweight and want to lose 5lbs or more, celebrate. If you worry and fuss and berate yourself for not being perfect and choose to honour yourself instead, celebrate each time you do that.

Appreciative inquiry (AI) is a healthy way to look at the positive progression in our lives. AI is about valuing where you are and the act of recognizing the best in you or the world around us, affirming past and present strengths, successes, and potentials that bring you alive. If you are a five out of ten in something important to you, allow yourself to feel "solid ground" around getting to that five and then lean into six, then seven.

To enable our best:
- Consider rest, fuel, movement, and mindset: they matter a lot.
- Think about or write down two things about each that you do pretty well.
- For each of the four domains, think about one area of opportunity for you.
- Of the four opportunities, select at least one you want to work on for the next week.

- Allow yourself to celebrate successes. If you miss a day or have a few more chocolate-covered almonds than you planned, go easy: consider that a reminder, not a failure.
- Keep coming back to the inspired intention without judgment. Celebrate wins often.

Seek aliveness. It's better that way!

Insight Ten:
Listening

Listening ... It was just a game. Or was it?

Summary: Listen more = richer connections.

Recall a time when someone thoroughly listened to you. How did it feel? Do you remember a time when a person didn't listen and how that felt?

I had been a guest speaker in the Moody's (CSI) Effective Manager Seminar in Toronto for several years. My hour-long session had two topics: Managing Risk and Thriving at Work. I found the receptivity to re-learning thriving such that I ended up doing more like 50 minutes on that. To speak to the opportunity for a great work environment, I began to insert a listening exercise midway through each session.

Here is how it went:
Part 1: One person speaks about something significant to them: an accomplishment, a dream goal, kids, work, for 1 minute. The other person listens, is present, has good eye contact, and doesn't speak. Then switch.
Part 2: One person speaks about something significant to them: an accomplishment, a dream goal, kids, work, for 1 minute. The other person acts

as distractedly as possible without leaving the room. Switch.

In the debrief, I asked how people felt. Here are typical responses:

Part 1: "Felt validated, engaged, connected more to the other person, felt I liked the other person more, wanted to tell them even more, encouraged, understood. I enjoyed it."

Part 2: "Felt like stopping and not saying anything more, felt angry, frustrated, not connected, not listened to, dismissed, not heard, guilty for wasting their time, stressful."

It was just a game, yet the participants' hearts and minds didn't feel it was.

Consider this communication and connection opportunity in the context of leadership and value in sales. Imagine the high productivity, rapport, and trust built by listening so well they can feel it.

The response I heard in those sessions that struck me most was people saying they felt like stopping and not saying anything more. This response was typical in every session I did. Imagine the loss of connection and the quiet hurt when someone doesn't listen to you. What was not said? In part, disengagement at work is because people don't feel heard.

A child, a spouse, a colleague, or a client will experience those same natural responses. One of our deepest needs as humans is to feel connected. Being listened to is a signal of worth, acceptance, and connection.

A relative of mine was a Jesuit for about 70 years. I went to see him quite often in the last stage of his life. When I spoke, I noticed his posture was upright but not stiff, facing me fully. His palms were facing up, upon his knees: as if receiving with open hands and heart. I always felt special. Many people did. Coincidently, Bill got an astonishing number of Christmas cards from people around the world he had touched.

Years ago, an Advisor I was Branch Manager of came to me in frustration about his low closing rate. I asked him to tell me about his prospect meetings. He told me how he let the person know all about himself, his accreditations, his skill at managing money, and his life outside of work. After listening, I suggested he not do that anymore and, with some skillful questions, allow the prospect to speak freely. Things improved considerably.

Our ego can interrupt others with the intended benefit of the immense wisdom we have to offer.

"I remind myself every morning: Nothing I say this day will teach me anything. So, if I'm going to learn, I must do it by listening." Larry King

Maybe now, with so many people physically disconnected, it becomes even more important to be a good listener, which naturally brings us closer.

Everyone has a story to tell—people matter. Listening helps. Here is a piece on active listening. https://positivepsychology.com/active-listening/

Listen well. It's better that way!

Insight Eleven: Gratitude

Thank you Mr. Wattles. I am grateful.

Summary: Gratitude is like free leverage on life. All gains. No downside risk: guaranteed. No disclaimer is required.

In early June, I started back to a gratitude journal listing five things I am grateful for each day. It's powerful.

The other morning, I reflected on the previous day, searching my mind for something that stood out. Finally, it occurred to me that several people helped me with various things that I was grateful for: two independent online queries about products I had purchased, and both people were super helpful and a great grocery store employee. And the oranges I bought, who picked them off a tree so my family and I could enjoy them? Then I found myself wondering who brought in all the food to the store? I figured that at least three people would get my car back on the road when I took my car in for service. And on and on it went.

How many people on any given day help us with little and big things that we are so accustomed to that we can easily take for granted? A friend of mine suggested there should be a new holiday called Interdependence Day. Nice!

But why think about gratitude?

A University of California, Davis study of 1,000 randomly assigned adults who practiced gratitude were happier, spent more time exercising, were better at regular medical checkups, took more preventive health steps, were more energetic, alert, and enthusiastic. Emmons & McCullough. (2004), The Psychology of Gratitude. Oxford Press.

Gratitude and acts of kindness create an upward emotional spiral. And appreciation tells the body, "Good things are happening to me!" Positive Psychology, Flourishing Center, New York

Wallace Delois Wattles (1860–1911) was considered a very successful "New Thought" writer and wrote a few great books. In one of his books, he devotes a chapter to gratitude in which he discusses his view of the attractive mindset of being grateful. To quote a few of his comments, "You cannot exercise much power without gratitude, for it is gratitude that keeps you connected with the Power." And a neuroplasticity truth is, "The grateful mind is constantly fixed upon the best; therefore, it tends to become the best; it takes the form or character of the best, and will receive the best."

Sometimes we live in the grind of our daily to-do list. And maybe gratitude for what is right and good in our lives isn't on our minds; instead, we dwell on what should be. And we can easily drift into rumination and self-condemnation. But living in that grind is to dishonour what is good, and there is always some good.

But I know there are painful and disheartening times we all experience, like the ill health or death of a loved one, divorce, personal injury, or a job loss. While it may be challenging and take time, gratitude can play a beneficial role in reducing the suffering from these painful events by broadening our perspective. We can feel loving gratitude for lives lost but that have impacted us, for partners that have for a time, shared part of a lifetime, remind ourselves to appreciate a body that is healthy and crazy amazing or for lessons learned and what a job lost had given us.

A good friend of mine sent me a note this morning and coincidently commented, "I am reminded to be in gratitude for what is in front of me and not be transported into mental worries of what or what not awaits me."

Consider:
Writing in a gratitude journal daily or at least once per week. "I am so grateful for ...."
Saying to someone how much you appreciate them and how much they matter to you like a spouse, a child, a parent, a co-worker, a client. Thinking it doesn't count.

If you have people working with you, it's helpful to tell them how much you appreciate all they do: this brings us closer.

"Piglet noticed that even though he had a very small heart, it could hold a rather large amount of gratitude." - A.A. Milne.

Dwell in gratitude and appreciation. It's better that way!

Insight Twelve:
Mindfulness Part One

Summary: Being in the present moment and knowing it. It is to be in a mindset of curiosity about our thoughts that arise naturally instead of self-judgment.

So much to say, so little space. Just like wine and time. Practicing mindfulness depowers the amygdalae (we have 2) and empowers the prefrontal cortex. That's the way that that is.

Our amygdalae are involved with processing memory and emotional responses like fear, anxiety, and aggression. Our prefrontal cortex is behind our forehead and deals with decision making, social behaviour, and orchestrating thoughts and actions related to our goals, otherwise known as executive function.

Mindfulness meditation is the practice of paying attention to our breath, so distracting thoughts become less dominant. Our brains, wired for distraction, have a negative bias. Both were very successful survival traits but only serve app developers and the media now.

When meditating, we will inevitably get pulled away by a thought. When we notice the distraction, the act of regaining our attention back on our breath is the chin-up or push-up for our wiring to our prefrontal cortex or "self–regulation strength." There is an abundance of information on mindfulness you can explore should you choose to.

A few apps I like are Calm.com MUSE: The headband; another great one is Headspace.

I have been practicing mindfulness for about five years. My observations:
- Immune system and general health - I used to get run down and get colds. Now I can't remember the last time I felt sick.
- Awareness - I have had a significant increase in awareness of how I feel and my thoughts and how they affect me.
- Reactivity and openness - A significant reduction in reacting emotionally (outwardly or internally), and that angst or anger duration are minutes vs. hours.
- Less judgmental and more open to diverse thinking.
- Compassion & Happiness – Much more caring of me and others, and I often feel good much more often.

These observations align with the research findings.

Mindfulness by another name. You could call it attention training or brain hygiene or mental rest and relief.

A few years ago, my wife's young cousin, once removed, and I walked along a city trail leading to a big park. As we walked along, he said, "There are a lot of birds' nests in these trees." I asked how he knew that. He said, "You just have to look up." So, we both walked and looked up to the big trees' tops, and he pointed out several nests. I had walked that path many times and never looked up. Now I do. That experience, in my view, is a form of mindfulness.

One could be experiencing mindfulness while doing a favourite activity or listening. I think bringing a mindful mind to how we show up in our various roles is not just possible but optimal. Mindfulness takes practice.

Going for several workouts gives us a feeling of increased fitness. Eating a healthy diet will inevitably feel good. Same for mindfulness: it's experiential. It's hard to tell you how you will feel if you exercise regularly or improve your diet. Practicing mindfulness will result in new and different positive feelings and insights.

The application to our work life is real: mindfulness promotes greater wellbeing on many fronts supporting resilience and pro-social behaviour.

The brain changes itself based on the environment and what we dwell on. Therefore, we gain a higher level of self-regulation by settling our minds, which supports our human capital's optimization.

One hundred years ago, if you saw a man run past your house, you'd assume he was chasing someone or chased. Now, people run and exercise in all kinds of normalized ways because of the known health effects. In time, mindfulness meditation will become a standard health protocol for reducing stress and increasing wellbeing.

The proven benefits of prosocial behavior are quite profound such as reduced social bias, increased tolerance, and compassion, and whether it comes from mindfulness, we need more!

Consider some brain hygiene for a few minutes each day! It's better that way.

Insight Thirteen:
Mindfulness – Part Two Awareness

Summary: Getting better at paying attention helps build awareness of what's happening now to respond thoughtfully.

Time spent paying attention trains the brain to be better at paying attention: good or bad outcomes depending on the subject of attention!

Being mindful, paying attention to the present moment allows for greater awareness of what is happening. What am I doing, saying, thinking right now, and does it serve me or not, or is it even accurate?

"Between stimulus and response, there is a space. In that space, it is in our power to choose our answer. In our response lies our growth and our freedom." Viktor E. Frankl, Holocaust Survivor, and Author

Several years ago, one of my daughters was at a playdate. It was 8 pm, and I called over to speak to the other child's mother. We agreed it was time. I asked her to send my daughter home. "No," she said. Then she offered to bring her back. It was an easy walk. There was no crossing a big, busy street. Around the corner, one block south. No problem. I asserted that my daughter was entirely able to make her way home safely and asked again to send her home. "No. I'll bring her to you:' she repeated. My daughter. My decision. Right there, I decided not to like her anymore. I felt offended by her rejection of my judgment as my daughter's dad.

Stimulus. Response. Very little time to think it through sometimes. A quick, emotional response causes lots of angst, disparities, and violence: someone taking offense to another view. With lots of emotion, a client once told me that she would use all her inheritance if that's what it took to fight her brother's legal objection to the Will. They never spoke again.

For a year or so, I took on a "not liking her energy," keeping to a minimum any interactions. Coincidently, during this period, I started practicing mindfulness meditation regularly.

One day, I was walking my dogs, and I saw her at a distance with her dog. My immediate thought was to consider that she has had a tough time of late, surviving cancer, and her husband is quite busy at work, not seeing him around much. With zero consideration of my past feelings, I felt compassion for her.

Then it dawned on me that I had decided not to like her. However, that mental structure of disliking her now felt more like a passing cloud than a rock. I was curious and replayed the "offense" as if I was an independent third party.

What is the truth, I thought? For starters, it's unlikely she remembers or has been spending any energy on it. Second, I know we both love our kids, and she was probably looking out for my daughter because she cares about her. Third, at a high level, we shared a common interest in safety. I thought it was entirely safe for my daughter, and she felt it safer to have her taken home. Just degrees of difference, not opposing views. Jeez. Silly me. What a waste of energy. Good learning, though!

When we make judgments about someone, what do we know for sure? We are at risk of small and big miscalculations by responding emotionally. Did my neighbour set out to offend me? Of course not. But in my mindless and internal response, I wasn't open to her real intentions: a better sense of awareness would have helped.

In any interactions with others, practice awareness of what is happening now.
- Do you have a good idea of how you show up?
- Are you fully present and open-minded?
- Are you listening and speaking equally?
- What does your body language say?
- Is there an alignment between how you perceive the interaction and how the other person sees it?
- We want to say it was a positive interaction and know the other person would agree.
- Are you attuned to the other person?

"If then, I were asked for the most important advice I could give, that which I considered to be the most useful to the men of our century, I should simply say: in the name of God, stop a moment, cease your work, look around you." Leo Tolstoy

Pay attention. It's better that way. Still tricky out there. Some are working from home, alone, or in situations not so easy. Be kind to yourself and others.

Insight Fourteen:
Noticing

Summary: Getting better at noticing the bad can help shift to the good.

Some time ago, I was walking along that same trail near my house in the city where my wife's young cousin, once removed, reminded me to look up. The trail winds through dense woods on either side, connecting a residential area with a large park: the scenery could put me 100 miles from the city.

I felt like crap and certainly wasn't looking up. A whole-body low-energy feeling. Down on myself. Feeling like not much could get me pumped up. Like one bar energy instead of five.

Some little inspired thought fought its way to the surface, encouraging curiosity. That stopped me on the path just before the bend and bridge leading to the expansive park. It was like I had to stop to let a part of me off to survey the situation. Standing there for a few minutes, I entirely took in the feelings of the low, uninspired energy: like a full-body heaviness.

As if an observer was saying, "Ok, you feel like crap. Why is that, and is the feeling legitimate?" And the better question that came next was, "Is this how you want to feel?'

The why: I was tired as I hadn't had a good sleep the last two nights. I had a project that I was stuck on and didn't have the creativity to finish. Ok, facts: tired and a critical project unfinished without the ideas to finish it. Ok, I thought, "What else is true?" I started to list the things I had completed in the last few days and was a bit surprised; it was a good list.

That felt good to see the good. Then I looked around and took in the natural surroundings: building a sense of gratitude further powered the upward spiral.

"Hey, wait a minute, what is going on here?" I get to walk along this beautiful path in the middle of the city. And I've gotten a bunch of things done. Great family. Health.

Gratitude adds velocity to the upward spiral is a key takeaway.

Right, so enough of the bad, I now want more of the good. But not to deny or gloss over the cause of feeling down, I asked myself what I could do about it. By the way, this is such a great thing to do. You are walking around with the most sophisticated organized system for information storage and retrieval in the known universe of about 1,000 trillion connections, give or take. So it's ok, you can ask it what to do.
My answers:
- Finish the walk.
- Get a good night's sleep tonight.

- And then, an idea popped in that would help me with the project, and then I intend to carve out time after the walk to the finish.

I enjoyed the rest of the walk. Finally, I got home and finished the project, and when I was lying in bed with the lights out, I reflected on the day and felt great about the shift to good. The next day, I thought about how that happened and came up with this formula: 4N Shift.
Notice. Name. Nurture. New.

Notice how you are feeling.
- Practice noticing how you are feeling. Lots of emotions, and we tend towards negative ones. Be alert.

Name the feeling.
- I am sad, embarrassed, frustrated, weary, happy, amazed, grateful, or in awe.

Nurture or be curious about the feeling.
- What is the cause of sadness or happiness?
- Even for the positive emotion, I would suggest this has value, so you get to know the "formula" of what makes you feel happy, then you can do more of that!
- Take stock. I find it is a universal human trait to underestimate the effects of recent experiences. You might say, "I feel low, and it's hard to get motivated, and I should not feel like that."

- Perhaps you might find reasons for your state if you take stock. Indeed, this time of the COVID strain can be a significant cause of unease.
- Taking stock isn't about masking or hiding from negative emotions. It's about acknowledging them and using them rather than allowing ourselves to dwell in the muck, which has no utility except for punishment, which no one deserves.
- Whatever you would say to your best friend, say to yourself.

New as in new action:
- You have noticed a feeling.
- Name it, so now you know what it is and decide to help yourself take a new, more self-serving, and right direction.
- Often it just takes some self-care and compassion, like a good night's sleep, to regain one's energy and perspective.

This short exercise has applications in life at work and outside of work. It has an application anytime you want to check in with yourself and regulate and upgrade your feelings.

We are very hard on ourselves. So do yourself a favour and be curious and check out feelings to keep coming back to good.

<u>Understanding Positive and Negative Emotions</u>

Notice how you feel. It's better that way.

Insight Fifteen:
Acceptance

Summary: If something isn't what you wanted, accept what is, then do something productive about it. Skipping the first part is a choice, not in your favour.

Acceptance in human psychology is a person's consent to a situation's reality, recognizing a process or condition (often negatively or uncomfortable) without changing or protesting it. The concept is close in meaning to acquiescence, derived from the Latin acquiēscere (to find rest in). *Source: Wikipedia.*

Thankfully I ended up laughing—a welcome relief. One of my teenage daughters had four wisdom teeth taken out just the other day. She wasn't laughing, although she was pretty loopy in the recovery area for twenty minutes.

I had the directions on her icing schedule and antibiotics and pain meds. I was determined to make sure she did everything she could to recover well. It started with reminding her to ice regularly. "You should do it this way, my love," I said too many times. "Have you taken the pills at the right time?" The following day I woke her at 9:30 to get onto the "right" schedule of pills. Not thinking that she was up until 1 AM or later, she was mad at me. "I am trying to help," I reminded her with growing frustration. "Well, you are NOT helping! I am not on your schedule. I am on mine. You woke me up for no reason!" Then tears. I left mad that she wasn't doing it my way.

Then I took our two red labs for a walk. The younger one is not well trained, in my view. On most dog walks, I get frustrated that Chili won't do what I say. Then, when all is calm in a typical move, she launches back to a tree to sniff the base as the older dog keeps going straight. I jolt to a forced stop with arms outstretched in a second, holding on to two taught 6-foot leashes like some medieval torture.

Nobody is doing things my way today, and it's making me crazy.

As I was about to get upset, I thought back to my daughter suffering from tooth extraction and pushing my structure and expectations on her and how bad that went. Now I am being pulled apart by two labs only interested in their morning plan, not mine. And I think about the fight it was taking against these realities.

I then relaxed and laughed at myself. Then, as if sensing my relief, the dogs reduced their tension, and my arms popped back into their sockets.
My daughter has taken her medicine and done the icing working on her schedule: ultimately, she is recovering.

As a Branch Manager, an elderly couple demanded to see me and in my office. The woman proceeded to complain about the poor service by the advisor. "He didn't do this," and "he didn't do that." Unhappy, she went on and on. Unfortunately, things didn't go as she wanted them to. Her husband spoke up and argued with her about some of the details. As the argument intensified, they shifted to face each other and continued to argue with each other.

I leaned back in my chair with my hands clasped together behind my head. Then, after a bit, I looked at my watch, unclasped my hands, leaned forward, and interrupted them by saying, "Is this what you both do, complain, and argue? Is that your life? Then you die. Really?" I remember them turning back, front and centre, staring at me in silence. That ended the meeting, and they left.

Hey, I'm not saying that if your steak comes rare and you wanted it well done that you say nothing, or if your hotel room smells of cigarette smoke, you should suck it up. I feel we really should speak up and honour our position. There is an opportunity to see situations and say rationally (with practice), "I accept that this is the reality right now," and then with solid ground under us think, "what can I do about it?"

Skipping acceptance is like running a red light. We don't have to like there is a red light or pretend we feel good about it. But there is a red light: a fact. So once there is a recognition, accept that reality and move to the most optimal next step.

"Happiness can only exist in acceptance." George Orwell

It all comes back to practicing awareness. It's better that way.

Insight Sixteen:
Resist Not

Summary: Notice resistance to what we want. Allow more, resist less.

In 1991 I attempted to swim across Lake Ontario in a world record time. The forecast was for light winds out of the west. But instead, a significant storm was building. I kept going up and over swells that grew to eight to ten feet in height. Finally, I got pulled out after 12 miles and 7 hours.

Sometimes things don't go as forecasted.

In the final stages of training for a second attempt in 1992, a friend suggested I see a channeler (someone who conveys thoughts believed to be from an external source or other consciousness) to get insight into the outcome. Stay with me.

We met at her office. She sat at a large desk, and I sat in a chair facing her. She asked why I had come. I said I had an event coming up in the summer and was curious if she had any insight for me. She closed her eyes, took a few deep breaths, and began to speak in a different voice. She said that if I focused too much on the outcome, it would be hard. But it didn't have to be hard. She said that if I just allowed myself to flow like a dolphin, it would be easier, and I would have a much better chance to succeed. An odd experience, but good advice!

It wasn't all easy, but I can attest that in the second half, I was in a flow state with singular focus and concentration with a sense of power in the water that felt amazing: like I was one with the water. First, I set a new World and Canadian Record. Then, two years later, I did it again eight minutes faster.

What do we allow ourselves to do, be, or have? And what part of our private or public vision do we resist?

A flower or a tree doesn't seem to resist its natural state of fully expressing its flowerness or treeness. For us, being in the zone or flow is a state of non-resistance. People in flow make it look easy.

We can move from enduring to enjoying or just feeling good by resisting less.

For a few years, my highest private aspiration has been to write a book. I've told people I am writing a book. In truth, I was thinking about writing a book and making lots of notes, afraid to reveal my most precious thoughts.

"Playing small does not serve the world." Marianne Williamson

Resisting and not playing our biggest feels awful. Yet, somehow being aware of the resistance and why it exists has opened up answers and more allowing. Lately, I've made excellent progress, and that feels good.
Awareness again: resistance feels terrible, and allowing feels good. Good to know. Allowing is like alignment with our best.

Ways to allow more:
- Be open to where there is resistance.
- Notice resistant behaviours.
- Become aware of the feelings that come with resistance and allowing.
- Choose more thoughts and actions that feel good.
- Meditation is a proven method to reduce rumination and increase positive self-direction.

If we see a psychologist, they are likely to start with, "So what's the problem?" It occurs to me there should be a door across the hall where we could walk in and answer the question, "Tell me about how amazing and wonderful you are and what accomplishments you are most proud of!"

We could regularly take stock of all that good stuff to know these were times of little to no resistance, all allowing. Seek more of that. Love is zero resistance.

In the world of investment sales, the business I was in for many years, there is a grid that Advisors must get to or else. Then another. I know someone who felt immense pressure to get to the subsequent sales recognition level and did some illegal things to get there. His behaviour caused jobs to be lost and over $4 million in settlement costs and legal bills to be paid out.

I wonder if it would be better if there were a value grid instead. Like ensuring value is provided and getting paid based on the degree of value.

How much value can we be bringing to relationships? Maybe Advisors should be paid more if they add more value and help clients' money last longer than they do. Perhaps offering value is more aligned to dwelling in the good for everyone. Maybe, in consequence, everyone would make more money.

Here's a brilliant example of flow. Over seventeen thousand singers come together over ten years in harmony as one voice. Disclaimer: if you choose to listen to this, I suggest you do it during an intentional quiet few minutes. It made me cry. Virtual Choir 6: Sing Gently

Seek to enjoy instead of enduring. It's better that way.

Insight Seventeen:
Choice

Summary: Choices are cumulative. Choose well.

"The life of every man is a diary in which he means to write one story and writes another, and his humblest hour is when he compares the volume as it is with what he vowed to make it." J.M. Barrie, the author of Peter Pan.

I think the moral of Peter Pan is to believe in the love of family above all else, that it is real and Neverland is an illusion. I like that and also take from the story a reminder to be playful.

The best teacher to remind me to play is my eldest daughter. Years ago, after getting home from work late, I ran up to read her a bedtime story. Still, in my shirt and tie, I began to read. She reached over and flicked my tie. I was not amused and stopped reading. She stopped, and I started again. Then she flicked it again. Finally, in a huff, I told her that I would end the reading if she didn't stop. Yikes, that's unpleasant to admit.

She looked up at me and said, "Dad, I was just playing." My response was, "thank you so much, my love, for reminding me how important it is to play."

Play is one of many choices that will show up in the story I aspire to have unfold.

We make choices all the time—all day long. But, ideally, there is some consistency or alignment to what we want at a higher level.

What do we want? Really. What is the life we mean to write and have unfold in front of us?

Clarity helps.

When I was about 17, my dad gave me an old book called The Magic of Believing by Claude Bristol. At the time, I was swimming competitively and trained 11 times a week, aspiring to compete and perform at a high level. One such opportunity was making the Canadian Team go to New Zealand later that year for an international meet. The book that I still have is full of examples and exercises on how to achieve one's dreams. On page 86, there began one activity that got my attention.

The prompt for the activity was, "what do you desire above everything else?" The next step was to write concrete goals, the answer, on a small card, like a recipe card, and then refer to it often.

The best shot I had to qualify for the Canadian Team was in the 200-metre freestyle. So I got the qualifying time, broke it into four timed splits that Iwould swim every 50 metres, and wrote them on the card.

When I looked at it, my first thought was, "I have never swum that fast and don't think I can do it." I kept looking at the card over the days and weeks ahead and kept training hard. Then, one day, I looked at my card and thought, "wait a minute; I have swum as fast as or faster than each split in a 50-metre race. I just had to put four of them together." It began to seem possible.

I was in lane eight at the qualifying meet. I felt ready: at ease, focused, and quiet in my mind. The timer asked all swimmers to take their blocks. I mounted the starting block and moved to its front, leaning down, awaiting the gun start.

My start was perfect, and the first 50 metres felt great. Each flip turn propelled me closer to the finish: this was the most effortless swim of my career. When I touched the wall, I didn't need to look up to the electronic timing board to confirm what I knew.

I went back to speak to the coach. He congratulated me on my personal best time and told me I had made the Canadian Team to New Zealand. I then checked my splits and found each one to be exactly the time I had written on the card, except the last one, which was two tenths faster. The trip was an incredible experience.
One's desire and intention, and clarity, if aligned with effort, works well.

From a Harvard Business School on goal setting:
- Eighty-three percent of respondents had no goals.
- Fourteen percent of respondents had plans but had not written them down. The study found that this group was ten times more likely to succeed than those without any goals.
- Three percent of respondents had written down their goals. They were three times more likely to succeed than the group that had some plan in mind.

The Psychology of Writing Down Goals

With goals, choices are easier to make. The right decisions can be about small or big plans: what to eat, what to say, what to get done, how to show up. Not easy all the time. But something done well, the right choice,is very different from nothing done. I choose to go for a run, or I don't.

Next week I will start a three-part series called, enVision, enRich, enJoy.

In the meantime, what do you desire above everything else? Oh, and write that answer down!

One of the best feelings is standing in the reality of that which was once a dream. Good choices make that happen.

Insight Eighteen:
enVision

Summary: "What do I want" is an excellent question. From here to there is attainable.

Sometimes we wish things were different: level of success, weight, diet, a partner, money, happiness. The most unhelpful part of this is getting stuck in rumination where there is very little utility. At worst, rumination leads to a downward spiral. That doesn't feel good. At best, we can acknowledge these thoughts and pick out learning and goals, thereby ending the seemingly endless loop. Essentially saying, "What are we going to do about it that helps?"

I like the word vision. A friend told me the other day that some people don't like the word vision and that they only want to think about where they are now and where they want to be: it sounds like vision to me. Maybe he assumed "vision" is necessarily big, all-encompassing. It can be; it doesn't have to be.

Naturally, people look ahead with hopes and goals and generally to be better somehow. Growth is a natural condition; that's why it feels so good.

However, I have observed a few challenges in moving from where we are and attaining our goals. First, clarity can be a challenge: getting it down to what we want. The second part I have done, and others have, is to dishonour our progress by focusing on what didn't happen: not good enough, not fast enough, not soon enough. And the final challenge is simply the ability, the gift of acknowledging the progress made or the goal completed, which sometimes we don't do.

High performers can have horizon thinking; they get little or no satisfaction from progress because they feel there is always more to do, be, or have. But, of course, the illusion is that there is no horizon. Joy can only come from looking back to appreciate the progress. Joy feels good.

Here is a practical, evidence-based goal attainment process I call enVision, enRich, enJoy.

A vision could be losing weight, an important business goal, shifting thought patterns to be more helpful, a big giant, audacious life vision, or eating less sugar today. Big or small, it will work for all: from where you are to where you want to be.

Briefly, enVision is about writing out a goal. The second part, enRich, speaks to dwelling on those micro-movements that have been done and aligned to the plan. And the third part, enJoy, allows for the practice of feeling good about what we have done: feeling joy and celebrating the little and big things done, which feeds further progress.

Part One: enVision

"I knew I had sub-four minutes inside me, somewhere." Roger Banister

That quote isn't necessarily about breaking a world record but don't let that hold you back! I think that quote is more about all of us listening to that inner voice of possibility, aspiration, and trusting the "voice" for that better something we want.

There are few things as fulfilling as being in the reality of what we once envisioned. And this ability to create our future is not restricted to a few or only comes by chance: our birthright.

The Miracle Question (*credit to Insoo Kim Berg*)
Suppose tonight, while you sleep, a miracle happens. The miracle is that what you want to have, be or do has happened, just like that. But you don't know about the miracle since you were asleep.

Remember, the miracle could be losing weight, a business goal, shifting thought patterns to be more helpful, a big giant audacious life vision, or eating less sugar or the new job you get offered. Big or small.

- How will you realize the following day that this miracle must have occurred?
- How will you feel?
- What will you be doing? What does your day look like now?

- What will be different?
- Who might notice that this miracle has happened to you?
- What will they see that is different?

Activity:
- Use the above prompts to write notes in a journal (higher connection to the positive neuroplasticity effect we seek than typing).
- Write for about 20 minutes for three days in a row. You might think your miracle (goal) is clear and straightforward and doesn't need 20 minutes. The point is that more detail better supports the new neural pathways we are creating.
- Freeform notes are perfect. Don't worry about perfection and grammar: bullet points are great.
- You might find using "I am ..." helps. Just let it flow.

"The best way to predict the future is to create it." Abraham Lincoln

Next week, enRich.

While we are looking at envisioning our best future, here is a good piece for our eyes Prioritize Your Eyes

Insight Nineteen:
enRich

This is the second of a Three Part Series: enVision. enRich. enJoy.

Summary: Dwell on that which aligns with your desired outcome: It only takes 12 seconds to start a new habit.

Overview of a three-step process for positive personal change:
enVision is about writing out a goal in as much detail as possible.
enRich is about dwelling on micro-movements: good facts and that which is in alignment with the vision.
enJoy is about the practice of feeling good about what we have done, which feeds further progress.

Imagine a walk. Let's say you are walking along a paved, quiet country road. You know this route well: kind of unconscious by now, and it gets you where you've been going: the same destination.

One day, something inspires you to go another way, a different way. You feel something is amiss for you on the regular route, which compels you to consider a new path. You feel a desire for more satisfaction or fulfillment. You wonder if there is a different way to a better destination.

To your right is a field. Something inside you tells you that going across this field may be that better way. You choose this new route and walk across the field. Looking back, you see somewhat of a trail from walking through the tall grass. You get to a new and improved destination.

The next day you are traveling the same route to the old destination and come to the point where you turned right to cross the field. You pause to consider taking the traditional way or the new one? Thoughts flood your mind of "maybe it's better to keep to the regular route? Comfortable. Safe."

Then you reflect on yesterday's right turn. Your thoughts become expansive, "it was a nice walk: scenery and perspective I had never seen before, I got there in better spirits. I felt an elevated sense of courage for honouring the voice inside me that wanted something different. I got there faster." For the second time, you turn right and take this new route.

The next day, you pause only briefly at the juncture. Each day you feel better and better about your new choice and find more reasons why this new route feels aligned with the place you intend to go. You feel happier, more fulfilled. After several days, the path gets more comfortable. The way is now a trail, and there is much less resistance from what was tall grass.

On another day, you notice how well-worn the route is. The next day you are surprised that someone has paved the path, and it is now a road. On another day, you see signage directing you to the right, so you don't have to think about where to turn: this indeed a much better route.

You once tentatively tried this route from an impulse deep in your heart that you are now taking unconsciously: having traded this much better route from an old pattern. That was a good trade: an upgrade.

The brain changes itself, for the good or bad, with repetition and environmental influences: this change is neuroplasticity, and fortunately, in this story, it was all to the good!

Donald Hebb, a Canadian psychologist (1904-1985), coined the phrase "neurons that fire together, wire together" to describe how the brain works throughout our life. Our brains are not fixed but malleable.

Paying attention to our vision, the micro-steps along the path to attaining the vision build new neural circuitry or, if you like, a new habit. For example, Dr. Rick Hanson, an American psychologist, has discovered that it takes about 12 seconds of attention and enriching an experience to begin to build a new pathway to the prefrontal cortex, where self-regulation resides.

Paying attention matters to goal attainment, and neurologically is just like a push-up to building a muscle: and like building a muscle, repetition is vital.

enRich

Definition: Improve or enhance the quality or value of something.

Synonyms: enhance, make richer, improve, augment, upgrade, reinforce, elevate, and intensify.

Activity

- Bring to mind the change you seek, the vision, or where you want to go or do or have: little or big.
- Ideally, you have written in detail about it or have it on a card.
- With a raised level of awareness, take a few deep breaths and long exhales each day and reflect on actions you can take aligned to the goal.
- Reminder: No amount of self-criticism and dwelling in the deficit of things will move us closer to where we want to go.
- If only one step towards the goal, celebrate that.
- Dwell on each step or experience you did for at least 12 seconds.
- Honour what you did.
- The noticing of what you did do and the feelings of accomplishment will become easier.

- The reality you are seeking will be drawn closer: that is the science of it.

Enrich your moments of forward progress. It's a smoother ride.

Insight Twenty:
enJoy

This is the Third of a Three Part Series called enVision. enRich. enJoy.

Summary: Seek out joy. Feeling good is better than feeling bad.

Overview of a three-step process for positive personal change:
enVision is about writing out a goal in as much detail as possible.
enRich is about taking action and dwelling on micro-movements: good facts aligned with the vision.
enJoy is about the practice of feeling good about what we have done, which fuels further progress.

A friend of mine is a high-performance tri-athlete. His training is more demanding than most, and he loves to compete. He lives nearby. I swim well, so he occasionally asks me if I want to go for a training swim with him at his club. A year or so ago, he asked.

I know he is in great shape. Better than me. I was once in excellent condition. In my head, the comparisons start: with him and me and me and past me. I joke around about him being much faster, and he kindly jokes about just hanging on to my speed.

Knowing he will crush me at my fitness level, I set up some disclaimers like I haven't swum in a while and won't do his proposed workout. He encourages me to feel capable of the training set ahead. I feel defeated before I get wet. I feel this sense of obstruction like I'm getting in my way: not a good feeling.

As he gently prods me to step up, I decide to say that I will go but don't want to feel competitive and do what I can and if he passes me, so be it. So I went, and we swam together. Mostly.

What happened was stunning to me. I enjoyed the swim. A lot! So did he. A lot! There was a sense of freedom and fun—no expectations of not being good enough, which, ironically, allowed for having a powerful workout. I felt elated afterward: joyful. And so did he.

I wanted to feel good, and locking onto thoughts that I was not good enough or fast enough was like a setup for misery.

Not good enough, fastest enough, highest enough, didn't meet the goal, didn't meet the hurdle, not smart enough—so much of not good enough we heap on ourselves sometimes. There is no joy on that journey.

Let's say joy and happiness are a destination we seek—two buses leaving the station simultaneously. One bus regularly stops to take in the view of the progress made and the road ahead, to experience each stop like a destination unto its own. Each stop the bus makes becomes a short moment to be present and restored with a short rest.

The other bus takes a roundabout route, detours around these stops; the driver believes that joy and happiness can wait and can't stop now. No time. Too busy.

The first bus arrives, realizing that although the destination was joy and happiness, the driver and passengers experienced joy and happiness many times along the route.

The second bus ran out of gas, taking all the detours, and only experienced the postponement of joy. No amount of joylessness will get to more joy.

Some people set big goals. I hope they exceed them. Maybe they meet them. Perhaps they don't. Big is better. However, some high performers only look ahead to what is next or what is unaccomplished. Like getting to the "horizon" only to find there is more to go. Not good enough. Always more. Many of us focus on what is wrong, what it should be like, what we didn't do, or what someone did that stopped us. Some of us live there most of the time. There's no joy in that. Finding joy is better.

In this third step, enJoy, these points help to nurture more joy:
- Acknowledge the experiences and small wins aligned with the vision.
- Accept that you created these new experiences and take ownership.
- Allow oneself to feel pride and joy at shifting your world towards the outcome you seek.

And more generally, do these to trigger more joy:
- Make a gratitude list at least weekly.
- Be kind. Seek opportunities to act with kindness.
- Show compassion, which should be a work word. Compassion induces engagement.

This direct route to joy is to honour that which is and done. That's not the same as being ok with not meeting the goal. Accepting what is, wherever that is, and moving forward from there, is healthier. Joy is a considerable energy creator and is like a doorway to expansion.

Chade-Meng Tan worked at Google. I read his first book, Search Inside Yourself. Awesome. I saw his second book come out called "Joy on Demand"; under-appreciating the title at the time, I thought, "Really? A book on joy, how much could one say about joy?" It turns out that there is a lot that one can say about joy—a great read. We deserve more joy, and more is accessible.

Joy is a feeling of great pleasure and happiness. So get as much as you can.

Insight Twenty-One:
Appreciation

Summary: "We must find the time to stop and thank the people who make a difference in our lives." John F. Kennedy

My teenage daughters say "awkward" when they feel embarrassed at something I've done.

I can't remember the place, but we were all at a store, and the lovely person serving us was East Indian. As we left, I turned to the lady, put my palms together close to my chest, bowed slightly, and said, "Namaste." I could feel it coming, "Dad, why do you do that? You've done it before. It's "AWKwarrrd," with a bit of ring to it.

While they knew I went to India for two months when I was 15, they hadn't heard my Namaste story.

My mother's cousin was a Jesuit priest for 72 years, and I called him Bill. Bill spent about 30 years in India, some of that teaching at St. Joseph's College in Darjeeling, high up in the Himalayas. I arrived late one night after a long trip from Toronto to visit. I plan on going back one day.

He loved sports and particularly swimming. They had a swim team and used a pool nearby. Due to

92

my competitive swimming background, he invited me to go over and coach the team for two months.

I went on a few excursions, like seeing the Taj Mahal. I saw tremendous wealth and also disturbing depths of poverty. Bill assigned someone from the school to take me to the Jaldapara National Park to ride on an elephant to look for the other four Big Five. I recall it took a whole long day traveling by bus connections to get there—jammed buses. Local people were traveling between villages. Hot.

We arrived tired and hungry. It was late, but the staff put together a meal for which I was very grateful. The staff cleared the dishes and directed us to our rooms. We walked down a hallway and soon came upon the kitchen to our right. The big doors were open, and I saw the people who served us our food, a chef, and people cleaning up. I turned and stood in the kitchen entrance, put my palms together close to my chest, and bowed slightly, and said, "Namaste."

I remember all the staff turning to face me and seeing their faces light up with smiles in that moment of being recognized. Next, I felt the hard grasp on my arm pulling me away, scolding me sternly for paying any attention to the staff, saying they were "nothing, nobodies, not worthy," and I should not have any interaction with them.

At that moment, I had a knowing: not thinking or considering or weighing up the pros and cons. A knowing like I have now of the love for my kids. I had a knowing that people matter and what I did was right.

My escort had grown up with the caste system and the term "untouchables," defining the lowest level of people in his country.

It's a core human need to feel valued and recognized. Evolutionarily it meant survival. People feel seen, heard, valued, and have a sense of connection when they are appreciated.

A great book on appreciation is called "Appreciate" by D. Stuart, T. Nordstrom, K. Ames, and G. Beckstrand. Results from a study were this message, "The most significant statistics from this research was that 37% of respondents identified recognition as the most important thing their company or leader could do to cause them to produce great work. That percentage was nearly three times larger than that of any other response."

When was the last time you heard or said, "Your work is of value, your contribution is appreciated, thank you."
"In the workplace itself, researcher Marcial Losada has found that among high-performing teams, the expression of positive feedback outweighs that of negative feedback by a ratio of 5.6 to 1. By contrast, low-performing teams have a ratio of .36 to 1."

Source: Harvard Business Review Why Appreciation Matters

I hope this note inspires you to say some words of appreciation to someone deserving of it. Remember, thoughts don't count; you have to say the words. Say to someone, "I wanted to tell you how much I appreciate all you do. Your work is valuable and matters. Thank you."

And appreciation applies to oneself: an appreciation and recognition of the gifts we bring to our lives. So you could say thank you to yourself.

When I went to India those years ago, I became familiar with Namaste's greeting, which means, "I bow to you." A deeper meaning of the bow is, "I see the light in you," a form of recognition of all that is good in the person.

To get the words out and appreciate someone or yourself doesn't have to be awkward. I bow to you.

Insight Twenty-Two:
Flow

Summary: Go to flow as much as you can.

Mihaly Csikszentmihalyi's friends and colleagues call him Mike. I am neither friend nor a colleague, but in case you're curious how to pronounce his Hungarian surname phonetically, it's "cheek sent me high."

You've likely heard the term flow. In 1975 Csikszentmihalyi did a lot of research into happiness and high performance. During his interviews, several people described their "flow" experiences using the metaphor of a water current carrying them along; therefore, Csikszentmihalyi brought that term into the current vernacular. This example from one of those early interviews tells the story, "My mind isn't wandering. I am not thinking of anything else. I am involved in what I am doing. My body feels good. I don't seem to hear anything. The world seems to be cut off from me. I am less aware of myself and my problems."

You've been in a state of flow. If you are a pilot, you've been in flow, flying high, a clear mind, no interruptions, and fully utilized skills. Or a photographer is becoming one with an image you capture perfectly or a golfer: that shot so effortless, dropping on the green just where you willed it, like magic—or paddling a kayak in challenging, entirely stimulating conditions. In nature on a hike. Or maybe just being fully present and engaged hugging your grandchildren.

There are many books about flow, two conferences coming up (below), and people in all walks of life, not just high-performance athletes, seeking to get into flow more often– so what's the fuss about flow?

At a minimum, flow is a state of happiness, and that's why Csikszentmihalyi started studying it in the first place. It is also a place of massive energy creation and performance. Or, as Csikszentmihalyi says, *"The holistic sensation that people feel when they act with total involvement."*

I related to a friend the other day about the second half of my swim across Lake Ontario and how, after a very difficult first halfway at 7 hours, I regained a singular focus and full power, finishing in a world record time. She asked how I could explain that. Flow was the answer; a complete alignment of body and mind absorbed in the task.

Have you watched a professional golfer or basketball player make a shot look easy? Have you ever felt that sense of ease and power all at once, a singular focus and feeling of joy, fully immersed in an activity? That is flow. And it turns out that flow experiences feel easy because the brain causes a particular part of the prefrontal cortex, the dorsolateral area, to disconnect temporarily while in

97

that state. That dorsolateral area is where our sense of self-doubt and the brain's inner critic are, and when disconnected, they get silenced, resulting in boosted states of confidence and creativity.

Also, activity in the prefrontal cortex (above your eyebrows) that calculates time shuts down while in a state of flow. That's why we lose the ability to assess the past, present, and future in a state of flow. This bit of super cool neurobiology is called transient hypofrontality: "hypo," meaning slow down.

All a bit like Scotty rerouting power from other sources to take the Enterprise to Warp 9.

When you move into a state of flow, some of our natural energy consumers shut down. Our built-in sense of time pauses, and our inner critic quiets right down: all things feel possible, happiness experienced, and performance maximized, the body and mind optimized.

We know from personal experience the performance model: if the challenge is well above our skill level, we freak out or give up. If the challenge is much lower than our skill level, we get bored. But the magical place is where the challenge feels possible and is just ahead of the skill level, within reach, accessible, and desirable.

Graphically it looks like this:

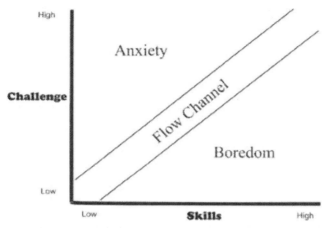

The Flow. After Mihaly Csikszentmihalyi, *The Flow (1990)*, p. 74

Ways to move into flow:
- Skill is well-matched and can stretch to attain the task.
- There is a clear goal or intention.
- No interruptions or distractions.
- There is a focus on the process, not the end state.
- Flow is about internal reward, doing stuff because you love it.

Engagement at work is a big deal for companies—annual surveys and efforts to raise it. Engagement and flow have common traits with outcomes of high performance. Flow can happen in any aspect of life and happens at work too. SAP, a German multinational software corporation roughly about the size of Royal Bank with about 100,000 employees and $43 billion (C$) in revenue, knows that every 1% in engagement score is about $60 to $80 million in net income. SAP invests heavily in its employees to optimize human capital because they know it matters on many levels.

When I think about flow, I think about non-resistance. Ease. I remember an Olympic swimmer and medal winner I read about that had a trigger phrase that popped him into a flow state, "easy speed."

Seek flow in your life. It's better that way!

Insight Twenty-Three:
Awe as an Antidote

Summary: Do stuff that lifts life satisfaction, like experiencing awe.

John Lennon wrote a song called "Nobody Told Me." He didn't quite finish it, so Yoko did. In 1998, she told a magazine, "I think that especially around that time he felt that again, the world had lost its course, its direction. I think that it's to do with, not confusion but starting to learn that life is always going to be a mystery."

One of the lines in the song is, "Nobody told me there'd be days like these. Strange days indeed -- strange days indeed."

I got a note from Air Canada yesterday saying they canceled our flights to and from our booked holiday before Christmas due to COVID. Ok, right, of course, tiny, tiny in the big picture, but I was sad about missing that experience with my family. Luckily the flights and hotel are fully refundable. So that's good but not great. It would be great if COVID cases worldwide dropped off a cliff, and our immediate and collective future looked like our past normal was closer than it appears now.

The WHO site shows 338,779 new COVID cases for October 8th, which seems the highest since this

101

began. I find that disturbing. We generally don't like uncertainty. Strange days indeed: from unsettling all the up to the well-documented human tragedy and deep economic distress. It would be less stressful if we knew the date it would end or when a vaccine would be ready for all.

So, what to do? Listening to the news and checking the stats and likely consequential low or high-level stress isn't an antidote. But it also isn't helpful to deny reality. That applies to any painful or disruptive event.

I was driving into the city yesterday and called my mom to check-in. She is still at her beachfront cottage on the shores of Lake Huron. She had just come in from taking pictures of the immense waves pounding the shoreline due to a super windy day. She cut the conversation short to go back out, catch the sunset, and get more pictures of the sun hitting the waves as they broke near the shore. At 93, sadly, she can hardly see but is out there being blasted by the wind taking video and pictures on her iPad.

I called her back later to listen to her thrill of getting some more great pictures. We talked about her being out there and watching the waves. She had a sense of awe, and we talked about that.

She said you have to be present to appreciate each moment fully. She mentioned she knows that each moment is unique, like seeing the waves. Each

102

wave is different. Watching the waves, with that sunlight hitting them just so will never happen exactly that way again. One time. Unique. Like every other experience and every other moment. No one experiences the same as another. Profound stuff.

Through that open and present mindset, one can squeeze out more rich experiences that line up moment by moment, day by day, add up to a whole and full life well lived.

Awe. There is so much one can be blown away by, and it turns out experiencing awe improves life satisfaction, provides health benefits, and makes people feel more connected. It sounds like an antidote to the effects you might be feeling from these strange days.

Eight ways awe makes your life better

My immediate family and I are celebrating Thanksgiving this weekend. Of course, not everyone celebrates Thanksgiving, but everyone can be thankful. Being thankful is also an antidote if you are troubled by this uncertainty.
For what are you thankful?
Take good care of yourself and be kind to others.

Insight Twenty-Four:
Pay Attention to the Body-mind
Connection

Summary: The body and mind are not separate. Know that to reach higher.

Do our thoughts influence our bodies? Or do our bodies' physical state influence our thoughts? Maybe both?

In 1981, Ellen Langer, a psychologist at Harvard, did something crazy. She took eight guys in their 70s who volunteered for her experiment, and she put them in a converted monastery for five days. Two had canes, and some walked in, stooped over. Everything about the inside of the monastery was set 22 years earlier, in 1959. Ed Sullivan on the black and white TV, Perry Como on an old radio, and magazines were available of the day.

Before they arrived, the researchers assessed dexterity measures, grip strength, flexibility, hearing and vision, memory, and cognition. While at the monastery, the men were treated like younger men and reminisced like their younger selves. There were no mirrors.

Afterward, and against a control group, the seniors were more supple, showed improved manual dexterity, sat taller, and their eyesight improved. In addition, independent observers said they looked younger than when they arrived.

In 2010, the BBC supported a similar experiment with six aging former celebrities. This time the setting was 1975, 35 years in the past. When the experiment was over, all the participants had marked improvements in various test scores.

On the negative side, thoughts can slow us down or stop us. You might have noticed thoughts connect to other thoughts and can create a downward spiral taking our bodies where the mind is going. Catastrophization is a state of mind that can be paralyzing. Being immobilized is a symptom of depression.

The mind is changing the body.

There has been a documentary recently re-playing made in 2018 called "You Are What You Act." The premise is based on new research from several leading psychologists into embodied cognition, meaning how our bodies' movement affects our thoughts.

"Fake it till you make it" might be a place to start but not meant precisely in this context. Don't fake knowing how to be a surgeon or a pilot, investing other people's money, or juggling flaming torches. The fact that Harrison Ford, Clint Eastwood, Kate Winslet, Jamie Fox, Ryan Gosling, and Tom Cruise (twice) have saved people from life-threatening accidents in real life are examples of heroic imagination. Just acting, but that acting transfers into real life. There is evidence that firefighters, police officers, and paramedics save lives while off-duty at a higher rate than ordinary people. This is because both groups practice engaging in dangerous situations for a living and are more primed mentally to act that way in real life.

The power pose was brought to attention by Amy Cuddy in 2012 in a famous TEDx talk. To date, almost 60 million people have seen it. Amy Cuddy TEDx Power Pose

She speaks about body posture and its effect on mood and performance. Expansion in nature is powerful, and contraction is weak. Standing full in our full height, shoulders back, arms extended at two and ten o'clock feels tremendous and creates positive energy. Two big thumbs up in the mirror will connect with a success mindset. Conversely, a hunched, inward posture will look weak and feel low in energy. Or head down and arms crossed trigger a closed, melancholy mood.

The body can change the mind.

Here is my point: we all have ups and downs, real-life stuff, painful times. We can minimize suffering. During the time of this writing, there was a second wave of COVID cases. Many people are distressed outwardly or inwardly. Some people working from home may feel at times a low sense of motivation or worse. Our minds have a natural negativity bias and are built for distraction to survive.

We can add strategies to our formula for resilience and sustainable performance or just a desire for more happiness by looking at the science of how body movement like posture can affect our thoughts and how our thoughts can affect our bodies.

Our bodies are not separate from our minds: all one and interacting and communicating all the time. The language of the body is feeling, and the language of the mind is thoughts and images.

At a minimum, a fake smile when you don't feel like smiling can nudge us to feel happier. Or a confident posture when we don't feel so sure can shift us to more confidence. Or acting like a hero can make us more like a hero.

By noticing our mental and physical state, we can provide the momentum to the mindset and direction to which we genuinely aspire through a bit of acting!

Maybe there is more at play than meets the eye.

Insight Twenty-Five:
Manwell

Summary: We've got more work to do.

Last week I had trouble writing my weekly Letter. It wasn't that I couldn't find the words but that I found too many and ones I didn't like.

It started with a goofy story of me trying to remember the lovely night cleaning staff supervisor's name at a building where I used to work. I came up with manwell as a memory trigger for Manuel. I felt like it was a creative connection to my thoughts and interests on how men can do their lives well.

I went to Go Daddy to see if I could buy the domain for future use of a website on men's health. I tried manwell.com, which would have cost me $7,000 at that time, so I went with manwell.ca for $19.99.

Early in my career, a man I worked with and respected died of a heart attack nine months after his retirement party. A heart attack is a form of cardiovascular disease and is 80% preventable. That stuck.

Then I looked into the fact that men die before women at every age. In some countries, men die on average as much as ten years before women.

Harvard Health makes a few points: Harvard Health
- Why Men Die before Women.
- Men take more considerable risks in life and generally have riskier jobs. More accidental and violent deaths than women.
- Men are more likely to commit suicide than women.
- Men are 50% more likely to die of heart disease than women (more estrogen in women may increase longevity).
- Generally, larger mammals die earlier.
- Men are less socially connected.
- Men are far less likely to make regular visits to a doctor.

Somehow this is where I took a wrong turn into a bad "neighborhood." While some of the mortality gaps are about uncontrollable biology, I became disturbed by the controllable, preventable stuff.

Now, with one click, anyone can get a list of what to do to prevent cardiovascular disease and live longer. Take better care and go to the doctor when you know something is off. Assume risk more skillfully to lower the odds of accidental death, so we don't leave loved ones sad and pissed off too. And stop killing each other. Enough.
Something triggered this downward spiral into stuff about which no one wants to think.

After men's health, I drove headlong into thinking about toxic leadership in corporations and the world stage. And then aggression, including sexual abuse.

I heard two leaders agree that certain employees who didn't meet a standard were a "waste of space" and overheard "we should put a bullet in their head" as a way to describe firing someone. Another leader used a finger gun to confirm the meaning. These were figures of speech but represented examples of an aggressive leadership tone.

The French Courts, in 2019, convicted seven male Executives of the French telecom company Orange with moral harassment for downsizing methods that resulted in 19 suicides.

A few years ago, Jeffrey Pfeffer wrote a book called Dying for a Paycheck. The introduction about the extent of toxic, stressful work environments and consequential human suffering made me well up.

Bob Chapman, CEO of Barry-Wehmiller, once spoke in front of 1,000 other CEOs (primarily men) at a conference and said, "You are the cause of the healthcare crisis."

His basis for that comment is that the enormous burden of health care comes from chronic disease. In addition, there is a vast amount of literature revealing chronic stress and other adverse health behaviors from stress. And the most significant source of stress is work.

It's not just that it would be nice to feel less stress; there are all kinds of terrible outcomes related to chronic stress, including dementia. Eventually, the body will say no. Employers should care about this.

The book "The Mind of the Leader" is based on extensive research, including assessments of more than 35,000 leaders and interviews with 250 C-level executives,

A note from the author says, "The world is facing a global leadership crisis. 77% of leaders think they do a good job of engaging their people, yet 88% of employees say their leaders do a bad job with engagement. There is also a high level of suffering in the workplace: 65% of employees would forego a pay raise to see their leaders fired." Mostly men.

Then I thought about world leadership: bullying, lying, corruption, and destruction and felt entirely depressed. Some countries' political systems, wholly run by men, seem fundamentally based on control, deceit, and lack. People want freedom and help to have a better life for their families. One of a few positives I can point to is Jacinda Ardern, the PM of New Zealand who recently won a "landslide victory." A media sound bite I saw called her "strong and kind."

And violence and racial injustice, it would take volumes to talk about it. There were protests related to the George Floyd killing in 60 countries outside the US. People want tolerance.

My daughters, who couldn't care less if someone was black, white, mixed, gay, mentally or physically challenged, rich or poor, are dumbfounded by intolerance.

A few years ago, when some high-profile men were exposed and convicted of sexual abuse against women. I brought my daughters together one night and told them how utterly wrong that behavior is in the strongest possible language. They must NEVER EVER allow a man to treat them that way.

Somehow it felt like I was holding onto an illusion that there is a third biological gender other than male and female, being nasties: a separate group of bullies, liars, tyrants, violent, racially-biased, and sexually deviant men.

I told one of my daughters, who is quite bold in her views of my challenge and observations about men, and she looked at me with one of those looks, "Are you just realizing all this now. Some men are a big problem."

I have started to read a book called, Behave: The Biology of Humans at Our Best and Worst. Two early points are that the brain's newest part, the cortex (behind your forehead), is where self-regulation resides. A study of monkeys showed that the larger the group they were put in, the larger their prefrontal cortex (PFC). More self-regulation, more measured, prosocial behavior. And secondly, the amygdala is highly responsive to stress. It triggers the fight, flight, fear, anxiety, and rage reactions: sometimes, our amygdala can get hijacked, and we react in uncontrollable, irrational ways.

Only for about 50 years have we known that the prefrontal cortex can be changed and optimized through attention training like mindfulness meditation, compassion training, and other methods. The effect of strengthening the PFC is to offset or depower the amygdala: more measured regulation, less emotional, irrational reaction.

Mindfulness is taught in every facet of life, from junior school to business school, first responders, the military, business, government, and sport.

Of course, not all guys are in that third group of nasties. There is an enormous outpouring all over the world of the desire for a better world.

Bob Chapman mentioned earlier, co-authored the book Everybody Matters: The Extraordinary Power of Caring for Your People like Family. Everybody Matters

Additionally, the book *"The Mind of the Leader"* offers a radical yet practical solution to the leadership crisis, "Organizations need to put people at the center of their strategy. They need to develop managers and executives who lead with three core mental qualities: Mindfulness, Selflessness, and Compassion.

And here is an inspiring example of a man helping to elevate the world. Lanny Cordola, an American musician, met a young Afghan girl whose two sisters got killed by a suicide bomber. Cordola founded The Miraculous Love Kids/Girl with a Guitar. Here they are playing Sweet Dreams by the Eurythmics. Afghan Girls playing Sweet Dreams

Okay, back on humanity's right side and the natural and inevitable progression to more tolerance and interconnectedness.

Insight Twenty-Six:
Sometimes the Energy is Unavailable

I have felt a bit unwell this week but went to a track to run some laps on Wednesday. I couldn't make it around once and felt my breathing strained. That was immediately discouraging and felt like a significant setback. Mad at myself, I couldn't get a run together, so I headed home.

I then decided to do something to feel better, so I had a sleep—deep sleep, as it turned out, after which I felt much better. Then, on Thursday, I went to the track and had my best run in a few weeks.

One day the energy was unavailable; the next, I was able to access it.

A few conversations this week and some reading brought closer a human behaviour of looking at what is wrong, not working, or being mad at ourselves for not doing enough.

Sometimes, the energy we need to complete a task, run some laps, or be creative seems unavailable. When we are not well, healing somehow, or emotionally drawn to deal with something, our bodies require a lot of energy.
Like a battery, we consume basic foundational energy requirements or drawdowns like being alive and moving around. Looking at what is wrong

115

consumes energy, making it unavailable, and looking at what is right, the reverse.

Our immune system is constantly working to move us to optimal health. When our health is compromised, more energy is needed, and less is available for running laps. Psychical healing is a stunning part of our biology, and we need extra rest to allow our resources to aid us. Emotional stress like caring for a loved one in need requires energy and can make less available for feeling vibrant and fully charged at work.

On top of our energy requirement under challenging times, looking at what is wrong doesn't feel good and drains our energy, but we can be mindful and, using a growth mindset, pivot to new feeling good actions. And learning to be better at noticing what is good or right or needed to feel better creates energy.

Focus on what is going right. It's all better that way. Inc.com Why it's better to focus on what's going right.

So, at this point, I will notice the good, like being with my family this weekend and in a few minutes after sending this to help my daughters put up a basketball net and that I want to get some rest; and all of that feels pretty good.

May you have a safe, fun, fabulous weekend in all the ways you want it to be.

Insight Twenty-Seven:
Truth Zone

Summary: If there's no evidence, it isn't true.

Once when I was a kid, my parents had a cocktail party and asked my three siblings and me to come downstairs and stand in a line to meet the guests. While we stood there with the guests greeting us, a tall man stopped at my younger brother, leaned in close, and, with a big booming enthusiastic voice, said, "Are you the swimmer?" My younger brother looked to his left and said, "No, he is." At "no," the man abruptly shifted over to me.

My brother was already a great soccer and rugby player. So he well deserved recognition for his achievements as much as I for my swimming.

I felt a piercing sorrow for what had just happened. For a long time, I held the image of a giant spotlight that illuminated my brother, then shifted to me, leaving him in the dark. I felt terrible he wasn't recognized, and I was. I felt bad for being good. This incident has affected me at times in my life, not wanting to be in the light because it might leave someone else in the dark.

My observation is that most people have memories of something someone said that hurt. Or something we needed to hear that was never said. Or an experience that left us empty and uncertain about our worth instead of confirming it. Needing safety and security and not getting it. Stuff that stuck.

The private world of self-criticism and the undeserving sentiment is not helpful. We might say things like, "I am not worth it, people won't like me, I am not enough, I don't deserve to be happy, or I am an idiot." Things we wouldn't say to a friend. These are all statements of lack reflecting the universal fear of not belonging or inadequacy: like being disconnected from our birthright of unconditional acceptance.

Limiting beliefs consume energy to hold and are depleting.

I am taking an 8-week course called Compassion Cultivation Training. Compassion means:
- To be aware of the suffering of another.
- Feeling concerned for the one suffering.
- A desire to relieve that suffering.
- A belief that we can help.
- A willingness to take selfless action.

We have all experienced that warm feeling that fills us by offering compassion.

There are three types of compassion: for others, ourselves, and the ability to receive it from another. Arguably the first, compassion for others is the easiest.

In the course, there are two weeks on self–compassion. Last night there was some discussion about things that hold us back from being happy or comfortably allowing a sense of compassion for ourselves.

According to Kristen Neff, there are three types of self-compassion:
1. Self-Kindness – Like you would show to a friend.
2. Common Humanity – we are all imperfect. "That person wants to be happy just like me."
3. Mindful non-judgment – practicing mindfulness nurtures non-judgment.

Kristen Neff on Self-Compassion

Self-compassion could be:
- Getting a bit more rest if we are tired.
- Improving our diet if needed.
- To take a little weight off.
- Beginning even in a small way to get more exercise.
- Practicing observing our mindset and moving away from thoughts of criticism and limitation.
- Being kinder to ourselves in little or big ways.

Here is some homework for the mind.

Limiting thoughts audit:
Ideally in 3 columns:

119

1. Make a list of limiting thoughts, beliefs, stories you tell yourself.
2. For each limiting thought or story, write down what you feel to be the evidence for it.
3. For each statement in (2), note down if this is true. Is there objective proof?

Do these limiting thoughts, beliefs, or stories help?

Truth zone (rewriting the truth)
- List a few things you have accomplished and for which you are rightly proud.
- Note some things you are good at and appreciate about yourself.
- What have people said that you do well?
- What makes you happy?

Review your notes and accept that these are all facts: this is the truth. The realities you have set out are in the truth zone: the place you want to dwell in as much as possible.

Summary: When we think, "I am not enough of something" or "I don't deserve something." we can ask ourselves if this is true or valid.

When I think back to that event with my brother, I can bring more truth to it: That man didn't handle the interaction skillfully, and it was not my doing. And the biggest takeaway is the illusion that there is limited light: it isn't true that one person is out of luck for another to have some. We can all shine at our best by the infinite source of light and our unique potential when we stick to the truth.

Empowering thoughts and true stories create energy and are expansive.

When we connect with self-compassion and think in the truth zone, we are on our solid ground. Instead of depletion, we find ourselves connected to an infinite source of sustainable aliveness. Through self-compassion, you become that source.

Be kind to yourself. It's better that way.

Insight Twenty-Eight:
All That Rushing Didn't Get me Anywhere

Summary: Slow down and get more life in your time.

Several years ago, which could have been on any given day, I felt like I had much to do. On that day, I was intent on squeezing in a lot. I had two chairs that I wanted to drop off to get restored at a place in the west end. I told the guy I would be there at 11 before he had to leave. Then I had to get back for a meeting. The chairs had been sitting in my living room for weeks, part of what felt like a never-ending to-do list: today was the day to tick this one-off.

As I left my house, I considered all the possible routes, estimating which would be best. "Cross country or along a busy highway?" I took the highway. It was slow as it turned out, and I wondered if I'd made a mistake. Then I got off the highway and promptly hit a red at the first traffic light. From there, I tried to maneuver through the streets, trying to avoid any more reds.

In the back of my mind was a clock ticking down towards the meeting I had to attend. I didn't leave much of a margin for error. Maybe this was all a mistake.

I was getting close, but if I aborted now, I'd be back in plenty of time. I hit another red. That was two— more stress. I turned right, thinking I could scoot around and through a side street to avoid some traffic. The light ahead was green. That decision looked like the right choice. Another green. Great. That's two.

The next light had turned yellow, and I thought for a second of hitting the gas and accelerating through what would be red very soon: I stopped instead but then felt more anxious at hitting these reds. As I sat there waiting for the green, I counted the lights so far: three reds and two greens. The ratio wasn't looking good. If I hit more reds, I'll surely be late.

Then a smile arose that turned into a laugh. I could feel the tension in my face and shoulders completely dissolve. I immediately felt more relaxed and noticed the thought, "Are you kidding me, tracking all the reds and greens you get in some big rush to the end while being stressed and almost driving through a red light? For what? Certainly not health and happiness." Who started this game of wanting to be proven clever at making the best choices and jamming an extensive list of stuff into a day?

At that intersection, I decided to enjoy the ride more. There was nothing about that experience that served me except for the awareness and learning. I decided to be a little kinder to help myself by allowing more time to get where I needed to go to lessen the stress and risk, and while I intend on being on time for things and filling my life with lots of good stuff, getting crazy to meet those goals doesn't help.

When the light turned green, I was still smiling. I took in where I was and glanced to the left to take in the view of Lake Ontario. It was a beautiful day. Feeling more relaxed, I drove calmly and safely to the furniture shop. I dropped off the chairs right on 11 to Gregory and got back in time for the meeting. It all worked out further, supporting the "trade" of all that energy consumed and stress and rushing for a better way to make future trips.

There is a road we're on, and it will have some reds and greens. The reds will happen, and no point in denying that. They can even be a time to pause and reflect. But the greens, I love the greens!

We have a limited amount of time and a choice of what we pay attention to and consequently the quality of that time. Therefore, we can have more life in our time by paying attention to the choices we make. Options that make the trip a good one.

May your road ahead have more greens and fewer reds and take care "driving" in the knowing that we are all on the road together. Enjoy the trip.

Insight Twenty-nine:
Human Capital

Summary: Human Capital, all we really have. What are we going to do with it?

A friend asked me about the meaning of human capital. Here's an example.

When I was 15, I spent that summer in India coaching swimming at St. Joseph's School North Point in Darjeeling, India, at the invitation of my mother's cousin Bill, a Jesuit Priest who taught there. The motto of the school is Sursum Corda, "Lift Up Your Hearts."

Bill made an appointment for me to meet Tensing Norgay at his office at the Darjeeling Mountaineering Institute. I entered his office, he sat at his desk, and I took the chair facing him.

We spoke for a while, but I remember his quiet confidence and understated nature more than what he said. He was a short man but had a powerful presence like it would be easy to believe he had climbed Mount Everest.

Subsequently, I met Edmund Hillary on two occasions in Toronto. Neither Norgay nor Hillary would ever speak of which of them made it to the very top of Mount Everest first on May 29th, 1953.

Hillary wrote some great books, a few I have; one is called "Nothing Venture, Nothing Win."

Two men fully optimized their skill, intuition, physical and mental strength to do something no person had ever done before: bringing "it" all up the mountain and using all they had to stand on the summit together.

We have collective resources: qualities, characteristics, strengths, perspectives, insights, and experiences. While it's good to be in touch with our resources, it's best to use them or express them at the highest possible level. Like the ordinary meaning of capital, money, it's good to have it but being held under a pillow doesn't do much good, fully utilizing it for growth is expansive.

And like leveraging money for higher gains, we can leverage our resources through cooperation and collaboration for even more good.

So, to me, human capital is our collective resources, expressing them at the highest possible level and the ongoing introspection and learning that allows us to expand further and optimize them for the good of all.

But sometimes, there is resistance or self-imposed thought barriers to unleashing our full personal power. We owe it to ourselves to explore anything that is keeping us from higher levels on our mountain.

Lean into the wind, navigate skilfully around danger or pitfalls, and push on.

Roger Banister once said, "I knew I had sub-four minutes in me somewhere."

To be clear, it's a relative game. I'm not suggesting we have to climb a real mountain or run faster than anyone. Instead, we can optimize what we bring to the journey, then more learning, more insight, and more expansion: from wherever we are to better is best.

Like Jake doing backflips down the aisle in the Blues Brothers, fully embracing the "mission from God." Let's accept that mission of a calling to higher levels!

I've heard this quote before from Mary Oliver, an American Poet that fits here, "Tell me, what is it you plan to do with your one wild and precious life. Mary Oliver - Short Beautiful Poems

May your unique human capital be fully expressed at the highest possible level.

Insight Thirty:
Patterns are Powerful and Weird isn't Always Worse

Summary: It's healthy to notice patterns: some help and some don't.

I remember coaching a triathlete to improve his swimming. While fit and capable, he had a flawed technique. The pattern or habit he learned was inefficient and chewed up effort. Of course, we have loads of great patterns like breathing while we sleep. But some patterns hold us back.

This triathlete swam the way he learned. But he was at the pool, nudged somehow, to the idea that maybe there is a different, better way to swim.

I shot and then showed him a video of his then-current swimming to assist him with a shift to more speed and less effort. Mostly, his ego thought he was swimming beautifully until he saw the video, like a mirror.

Then I told him how to change the pattern. He listened and did what I said while I videoed his new technique. I asked how that felt, and he said it felt a little weird and awkward. Then I showed him the video revealing a much improved, more efficient stroke. Feeling strange and uncomfortable wasn't worse; it was better.

"Everything is hard before it is easy." Johann Wolfgang von Goethe, Writer (1749-1832)

We couldn't function without patterns. Studies show that about 95% of decisions, actions, emotions, and behaviours are unconscious. Cells are in on the game, all 37 trillion cells or so of them.

Our cells have different life spans, some a few weeks, some several years. Our whole body is fully regenerated about every 7 to 10 years. The crazy excellent design is that the collective cell intelligence or patterns that help us ride a bike gets transferred to each new cell, perfectly intact. If you haven't ridden a bike in twenty years, your body doesn't draw a blank when you grab the handlebars. Cells die and regenerate, and memory is transferred to the new one even as you read this.

About ten years ago, I had developed a pattern of living with constant fatigue. I was stressed out, exhausted, and felt flat emotionally. One evening I went into the bedroom of one of my daughters to put her to sleep. She was six and sitting on the end of her bed, not ready for sleep. I asked her to get into bed; instead, she looked at me and asked if I was happy. I lied and said I was.
She wouldn't get in bed, and I got furious. I was looking at her that night as if through a window not cleaned in a while. I couldn't see her clearly—the madness of the effect of a destructive pattern. However, from deep inside, a nudge reminded me

I was looking at a miracle. My daughter. A human being. The most precious thing in my life. But in that pattern of stress and exhaustion, that miracle was so far away I could hardly see it.

That event was one of a few nudges that woke me up to change some patterns. So here is a **neat** acronym I dreamt up with the hope it helps.

Noticing - Let's assume the big goal is to be happy and healthy. What can we notice that gets in the way or doesn't help? Patterns around how we do self–care and private thoughts? How do we do relationships? Our career? Our communication style or biases?

Empowerment: We can change patterns if we want to. We can do stuff in different, better ways for a higher good. Our environment and what we choose to dwell on change the brain's structure through neuroplasticity to more great or more grind: we get to choose. With the right choices, more of our remarkable cells can, over time, get embedded with new upgraded versions of themselves for more great and less grind.

Awareness and Intention – Becoming aware of a pattern that doesn't help is like driving down a road and suddenly realizing you're not going in the right direction. Pulling off or even slowing down is a start to a better way. Once we've taken our foot off the gas, we can begin to think about what our preferred destination is. There are always places and times

130

on the journey to pause and reflect on our future intentions.

Transformation - Sometimes, it's inch by inch. Sometimes it's big and bold. Hold on like Velcro to the early changes. Celebrate little and big wins. Fuel the victories by shifting demeaning self-talk to be uplifting and encouraging. Move from reacting to responding. Be gentle with yourself in the transformation. A comfortable sense of ease is best. What can be a cause to celebrate learning, feel smart, and be grateful might be perverted by the ego to self-criticism for not seeing this until now. There is no way back. There is only forward.

Positive change may feel weird at first because it's different, not because it's worse. You may think this is easier said than done. But if not tried, it won't get easier.

May your patterns and habits continually be transforming for your higher good

Insight Thirty-One:
Is Kindness Coming Out?

Summary: Be not too busy for an act of kindness to yourself and others.

Recently I was speaking to a group about kindness and asked for an example of receiving it. One person recalled a close friend driving for miles to drop off some flowers when she was going through a tough time. I could tell from how she expressed the experience that it was a significant and lasting gesture.

To receive kindness from another person from a singular selfless motivation says the receiver matters. At the core of all human beings is the need to feel connected and seen: to feel they matter to someone.

But life is hectic.

In 1973, a large group of Seminary students was gathered together and given the task of preparing a talk on either their seminary jobs or the Good Samaritan story. Unknowingly they were part of a study on kindness. With their speeches prepared, the person in charge gave them different urgency levels to get to the other building for the talk. On the route to their address was a "homeless" man sitting against a wall in evident distress. In low hurry cases, 63% helped, in medium hurry 45% and high hurry 10%. Overall, 40% of the students helped the homeless man.

The study showed a person in a hurry is less likely to help people, even if they are on their way to speak on the Good Samaritan parable! Some of the students stepped over the victim on their way to the building.

One speculative conclusion was that compassion and ethics become a luxury as our daily lives' speed increases. Or perhaps more palatable, that in a rush, there was a narrowing of the student's focus, and they failed to make the immediate connection of an emergency. Rushing is stressful, and stress reduces peripheral vision, figuratively and literally.

The inflow of information and the busy world we've created often crowd out others. We can rush through our day thinking about our schedule, living internally. But living in a rush won't fully acknowledge the external world: those around us we are connected to and on whom we depend.

At the time of writing, the world is in the depths of the COVID pandemic. We are all in this together. Like no other time we have experienced, this period will benefit from more compassion and kindness: to ourselves and each other. We mustn't be too busy to stop and offer help in some form instead of stepping over others' struggles and distress.

"I shall pass this way once; any good that I can do or any kindness I can show to any human being, let me do it now. Let me not defer nor neglect it, for I shall not pass this way again." Etienne de Grellet, Quaker Missionary

A few years ago, I made a point of committing random acts of kindness and made notes on each of the 55 I tracked. As a result, I met Sacke, a man I saw crying, and found out his sister had died recently. And Cheryl, an Inuit teenager sleeping in an alleyway behind an office tower. And Bill, who some think was a University Professor and has been homeless for 20 years.

I learned that while I sometimes questioned whether to approach someone or say something, not once would it have helped to ignore my initial impulse to act or say a word or two because we cannot know how much a gesture of kindness might mean to someone.

Only acting on the thought makes it count.

Each time I stopped, I sensed the person felt a little better. When I was giving Bill a Starbucks card, I noticed someone watching with a big smile. The odds are very high there is a meaningful ripple effect at play in acts of kindness.
"Carry out a random act of kindness, with no expectation of reward, safe in the knowledge that one day someone might do the same for you." — *Princess Diana*.

In 2011, Orly Wahba wrote and directed an inspiring 5-minute video called Boomerang about acts of kindness's ripple effects. Watching the kindness is so inspiring that there have been over 100 million views so far! Kindness - Boomerang Video

Consider:
- Make kindness to yourself and others essential work.
- Practice COVID kindness – it's hard to know how people are doing through this.
- Pay ahead for someone's lunch or coffee.
- In speaking to someone, ask how they are doing.
- Give a compliment.
- Let someone go ahead in line.

And by being a little kinder to ourselves, we can sustain a higher capacity to help others.
Go ahead, make someone's day!

Insight Thirty-Two:
I Didn't Like Her, Then I Did

Summary: More alike than different.

At the first in-person session of a six-month course I took once, the 30 participants came in and found their seats. I was keen and headed to the front row. I approached the chair I was aiming for and noticed the instructor preparing behind the podium. In an instant, I decided I didn't like her.

Unconscious bias: an immediate feeling I couldn't explain that was unfair.

I felt like I had made a mistake in sitting upfront, now feeling uncomfortable instead of keen. The best I could come up with was the vibe that the instructor didn't like men. But, unfortunately, that unfounded notion somehow distorted my thinking about being in a primarily female audience, which made me feel a bit out of place and distracted me from the course I had been excited to take.

As the course unfolded, some of my classmates spoke highly of the instructor, and I would wonder what they saw that I didn't. The few casual remarks about her ex-husband as if we were girlfriends in her living room, I found off-putting. I asked a question at one point. How she let me know she didn't understand made me feel like she didn't like me either.

The course ended, and the material was excellent. Most participants were thrilled with the instructor: I only had a modest positive impression.

A year later, the class got invited to a talk she was giving. I went mainly to see the participants who had become good friends. In her introductory remarks, she talked about how women should be running the world. For the record, I feel that more and more women bringing their voice to the world in all kinds of ways is not only the right thing but critical for a better future for all. However, I also believe that some women and some men should not be in leadership roles.

I didn't stay long.

Recently I signed up for a two-day live online writing course, and one of the 12 participants was this person. The memories started scrolling in my mind like a video on YouTube. But before I allowed my bias to become fully reformed, I hit pause. As if a 3rd party observer, I rewound to look for any hard evidence to support my feelings for a few seconds. None. There was no hard evidence that she dislikes men in general or me in particular: no basis for the bias.
I stayed on "pause" to see if another story might unfold.

We would be in pairs a few times to discuss topics and share ideas. Then, as if expecting the reverse of the negative expectation I was dwelling on to help me, we ended up in a Zoom Room together.

We caught up a bit. It turned out she was pleased to see me. I asked about her ex-husband. She said he had passed away, and I could tell that was hard for her. Now I feel a sense of compassion. We talked about our writing projects. She thinks my book is significant work and generously gives me lots of feedback that cuts into her time. I feel grateful.

She has seen success, and she has had painful events just like me. She has views she feels are important and wants to express them, just like me. She wants to help people with her book, just like me. She wants help with completing her book, just like me. She told me she has struggled with being too hard on herself, just like me. Now I like her and don't know why I didn't.

The next day I sent her an email with thanks for the feedback and saying it was nice to see her. She responded, saying the same thing and wondering if I was interested in being an accountability partner with her.
I wonder where we have biases that don't serve us: assumptions taken as fact. A story that we choose to live that isn't true and we could rewrite.

My first unconscious impression separated me from her and blocked more value I could have received during the course. So I lost out in the bias.

But without the bias, we both will win, which means my life story and maybe hers will change a bit for the better.

"Don't carry a grudge. While you are carrying the grudge, the other guy's out dancing." Buddy Hacket

Even with one person, a little more conscious awareness that they might not be the story we have created opens up the possibility for a positive shift and richer experience where none existed.

Magic.

More alike than different.

Insight Thirty-Three:
Truce

Summary: Press on against any imagined foe. Celebrate every inch forward.

Most people thought the Great War that started in July 1914 would be over by Christmas. Instead, the fighting leading up to that December had ended up at a standstill. Both sides reinforced their positions by digging out trenches along the Western Front to live and fight and die.

If laid end to end, the trenches would extend for at least 25,000 miles. The trenches were as close as 35 yards, a third of a football field at some spots.

There was severe frost on the morning of December 24th, 1914, in France. The trenches were cold and muddy. By noon most shootings and shelling had oddly ceased. Letters home from both sides reported a "strange atmosphere" that developed. One side noticed coloured lantern light becoming brighter in the other trenches as dusk arrived.

In one section, as the cold night descended, a German Officer, Walter Kirchhoff, a tenor in the Berlin Opera before the war, began to sing Silent Night. The beautiful sound was striking against the devastation and darkness all around. Soon both sides joined in, inducing a sense of all things being calmer and a lttle brighter. Each side took up singing Christmas carols and shared words of encouragement, further brightening the atmosphere.

On Christmas day, Sergeant Fredrick Brown was the first to step out of the trenches unarmed and walk into "no man's land." Brown and others' initial apprehension gave way to a sense of shared humanity and peace that saw about 100,000 soldiers from both sides rise from their trenches in various sections and join together in the temporary ceasefire.

A German and British soldier gladly traded buttons as souvenirs. A British barber trimmed the hair of a German soldier. A German and British soldier hustled off to a farmhouse to find some wine to add to the festivities. A soccer ball appeared from the British side, and soon a friendly game ensued with no referee required. There were burial ceremonies and prisoner swaps. And the soldiers exchanged gifts of chocolate and tobacco. And soldiers wrote home describing the unbelievable truce and shared celebration of Christmas that had occurred.

Years ago, I went through a very challenging period as a Branch Manager. It felt like the office of salespeople were mostly bullies and bandits. During that period, on the way to work, I would quietly recite the Lord's Prayer as the only comfort

I could find that would keep me safe in what felt like a war zone. Then, upon arriving, I would go to my office and dig in, and leaving to walk around the floor felt as risky as sticking my head up over a parapet.

Sometimes I would worry about something upcoming and think it would be difficult or go wrong or be met with a challenge when there was almost nothing close to the imagined negative outcome: preparing for a battle when none existed.

"I've had a lot of worries in my life, most of which never happened." Mark Twain

Self-sabotage is little and big mental skirmishes that keep us from moving faster to our goals and aspirations.

Negativity bias is a natural condition that makes negative experiences more potent and "sticky" than positive experiences.

Catastrophization is a cognitive distortion where we jump to the worst possible conclusion without all the facts. We make stuff up that snowballs into an assumed crisis or conflict.

Sometimes we might even be self-critical that we're self-critical.

We must be vigilant about the saboteurs that can raid and rob our birthright of health and happiness

142

through their covert actions. So, if you see an opponent when you look in the mirror, consider calling a truce for the holidays.

Here are some tips for the truce:
- Be on alert for thoughts that don't help and turn to ones that do.
- Think and speak in a self-empowering way.
- Forgive yourself.
- Do things you love to do. Seek out your inspired self.
- Take an inner retreat of healthy rest, fuel, movement, and mindset.
- Write a list of things for which you are grateful.
- Be kind to others and your best friend to yourself.
- Write out your very best and optimal outcomes for the New Year.

And when the truce ends, try reframing the "battle" if indeed it feels like that sometimes, to a celebration of every inch of ground you can hold that is closer to your goals and aspirations.

There must be no standstill or digging in against an imagined foe. The only way out is through and forward, uplifting yourself every step of the way.

Insight Thirty-Four:
Overcoming the Challenge

Summary: It's been tough, but here is a way through.

While I was swimming across Lake Ontario years ago, at times, I felt alone, particularly in the troughs of waves and the cold, like I had one experience and everyone else on the crew was having another. But at a high level, we were all part of one event.

This past year each of us has had our own experience dealing with the consequences of COVID 19. But at a high level, we were all part of one event, albeit the most severe global event of our generation. So many people got sick, and lots died. So many people have suffered at the loss of their loved ones. So many people have lost their jobs. Massive disruption in so many little and big ways.

While all that is true, there are some other truths. Like heightened global cooperation, stunning technology to stay in touch and keep life and business moving as best we can. Many families spent more time together. We hope that was a good thing. In my case, it was a blessing. Vaccines are developed and rolling out, and the market has held up.

I've heard many stories of people taking better care of themselves and considering more deeply things that matter and for which they are grateful. And there have been countless acts of compassion and kindness to others. One of which stands out to me is the image of a lone musician playing a moving piece of classical music on a hospital's rooftop to acknowledge the health care workers there. A violinist plays to health care workers.

There was sadness in December for the restrictions on how people around the world may have traditionally connected. More people were alone. It's healthy to acknowledge our feelings of sadness. Sitting in gloom too long, however, will not make us happy or grateful or change things.

Hope helps and is part of resilience, at which we are pretty great. Scientists say 99% of all species that have ever existed are extinct. Yet, we are exceptionally good at surviving and thriving. Embedded in each of us is the capacity for thriving: some days (or years), it might not feel like it, but we all have that in common.

We also do kindness and compassion well, which support mutual thriving. So here are two books if you are interested in humanity's capacity for success through our innate goodness. I have read and highly recommend the first, and the second I plan to read Humankind: A Hopeful History and The Compassionate Achiever.

Hope unfurls aspirational "sails." Aspirations lead to intentions and then to goals. Aspirations are like being called to a higher level. It feels good to expand ourselves by setting goals and achieving them. Goal attainment is in our wiring. Growth is a natural state.

One of my goals is to offer you, through the following four Insights, personal and science-based strategies to create goals and attain them.

Starter thoughts.

Think big and act in small ways:
Someone once asked me how I could have swum 51km across Lake Ontario. My answer was that I didn't stop. Getting to the top of a "mountain" one step at a time is the reality of it.

There is capacity behind aspiration:
It doesn't make sense to envision a destiny and not have it within us to get there. Our world is full of completed dreams if we choose to see them. Some might ask for help from the universe or the place they see to be a source. You are the source. Some might ask for a bit of abundance as if there is only so much to go around. You are the supply.

"I knew that I had sub-four minutes inside me, somewhere." Roger Banister

Weight but not heavy:

146

Meaning and purpose are motivators. So when you are in deep and struggling with a goal, it's constructive to know your "why?" A good "why" has weight or power, real meaning, empowerment, creates flow and isn't a heavy burden.

Action:
I suggest you carve out 3 20 minutes journal sessions and ask yourself this question: "What is it that I want to create in my life? Then, allow yourself to be fully deserving of the answers.

And if you are down and struggling, consider this saying, "Fate whispers to the warrior, "You cannot withstand the storm." The warrior whispers back, "I am the storm."

May this New Year exceed your highest aspiration.

Insight Thirty-Five:
We're Going to The Moon!

First in a four-part series on goal setting and attainment.

Summary: It's best to know where we are going and how to get there skilfully.

NASA has a plan to send people to the Moon in 2024. But that's only the intermediate goal. The big prize is getting to Mars: this is big stuff and requires a massive number of small and big steps to get there.

We likely have other plans: more earthly goals. For example, we might want to lose some weight, get fit, be more focused, read more, be more diligent in our financial planning, or do some compelling work at work.

A goal could also be to feel a certain way, like rested, energized, or more motivated. Or maybe one or two words will help keep all the things we want to be aligned and flowing, like being present, disciplined, or courageous.

"Whatever you do, don't...." How we construct a personal goal matters to motivation and its attainment.

One of my longest-time friends was an exceptional swimmer. When he was 13 or 14, he came home from a swim meet with gold, silver, and two bronze medals. With great pride, he showed his father the results of his hard work. His father ripped into him for getting two bronze medals and told my friend he would have to do better to substantiate the money spent on one of the best swim clubs in the country.

After World War II, the science of psychology was primarily devoted to curing illness or lack. Taking someone from minus five on a spectrum to zero or "average" is called the weakness focus: what is wrong rather than right. I reported to a guy once who would point out things he didn't like about my work. While I believe he thought these conversations helped, the way he brought them up to me hurt and certainly wasn't motivating.

In the early 1900s, William James, an American Philosopher, began to look in earnest at optimal human functioning. The idea and study of all the stuff to the right of zero, say to plus five, has created the field of positive psychology, which is quite rich with research about thriving.

The science of thriving is a much healthier basis for setting and attaining the goals we desire to achieve. Here is a science-based look at goal setting structure:

1. Proximity – How far out in time is the goal to be attained? Shorter-term goals tend to

be easier to stay focused on and can be used to support longer-term goals.

2. Specificity – "I want to read eight non-fiction books this year" is more specific than just "to read more." Being particular helps our brains "see" or bring in that, which allows us to manifest our intention.

3. Orientation – "I intend to eat a healthy diet" (approach goal) is different from "I want to eat less crappy food" (avoidance goal). Our brains will focus on healthy or crappy, not on "less." Go with approach goals.

4. Purpose – As in the purpose of the goal. Is it to learn, develop a skill, or is it about performance? There are more positive outcomes with a learning goal and more negative effects or risks with performance goals. If we don't hit the target, we may feel like a failure or lacking. Be aware of potential negative mental feedback if performance goals are not met.

5. Duration – A "process" goal is a regular action, like writing three pages each day. These tend to be about creating habits: more effort to sustain. An "end state" goal is a specific task after which nothing is required, like, "I will finish writing the book."

If we put our goals through the above filter, we can likely fine-tune the intent to increase the wording's potency.

The other day I was tired. The last part of some amazing chocolate ice cream was in the freezer. I had intended to eat only healthy food that day, but fatigue and desire teamed up and overcame self-regulation, and the next thing I knew, I was rinsing out the empty container. I decided to forgive myself.

On a more serious note, we can decide to, and it's ok to, forgive ourselves for something we haven't done, become, or acquired yet. Of course, beating ourselves up for something not done is a nasty, twisted bit of wiring from which people can suffer. But, on the other hand, forgiveness might loosen up some energy to empower what we want to create.

Beginning now with awareness and learning from wherever we are with whatever level of capacity to move towards our goal is logical, a little kinder, and works better. And a little ice cream along the way is ok!

Insight Thirty-Six:
May the Wind Always Be at Your Back

_____

Second in a four-part series on Goal Setting and Attainment.

Summary: If you want to but don't think you can, figure out how you can.

The first part of this four-part series on goals uses the following structure to make them more compelling.
1. Proximity – is it short or long term.
2. Specificity – Detail and specificity are better than general language.
3. Orientation – Frame the goal in terms of what you want, not what you don't want.
4. Purpose – Know the purpose of the goal: to learn something or to complete a task?
5. Duration – Is the goal a regular action or habit (process), or is it a specific task after which nothing is required (end state).

My book coach gets these Insights each week. Right after the last Insight, I got an email nudge from her about the book I am writing. I have one big vision for seeing the book completed and have chapter headings and lots of words, but I am not executing consistently enough to have it finished anytime soon. That doesn't feel good to say out loud.

So I reviewed what I had just written about (!), looking a little deeper into what was going on. Two things became evident and real: (1) the goal of "writing a book" doesn't meet the optimal structure above, and I often get paralyzed by its bigness. And (2) I take on a lot: big, huge, multiple, and ambitious goals, making it hard for me to be on top of all of them.

When I was training to swim across Lake Ontario, I met resistance in my mind around the goal's magnitude. I recall realizing I was thinking over and over, "How can I possibly swim 51 kilometres?" That unchecked mind chatter was like a current running against my training efforts. I needed to do something different to turn the current around so "the wind" would be at my back. I brought logic and facts to bear.

I could easily swim 1,500 metres and would do a 10,000-metre work without too much trouble. So I changed my narrative by reflecting on what I had done that made the big goal more plausible. Then, later on in reflection, I took the "negative" thought or blocks as information to be curious about and reworded them to a position of strength, virtually eliminating the "current" against me.
The thoughts that were now emerging were about the speed I could do it in. Re-purposing the energy was like now going the right way on a flume ride!
Focusing on strengths and acknowledging successful training milestones supported self-efficacy, which is how well one can execute the

necessary action to deal with or achieve the desired outcome.

"Whether you think you can, or you think you can't, you're right." - Henry Ford.

Boosting self-efficacy to support goal attainment:
- Role models – "That person did it, so can I."
- Cheerleader- Someone (or yourself) that is fully there for you.
- Managing stress skilfully – This is trainable.
- Knowing your strengths - Write them down.
- Having mastery experience – "I can do this. I am doing this."
- Savouring wins – KEY: Dwell on small and big wins, good facts aligned to your goal or direction. Neuroscience research shows brain changes or molds to repetitive influences.
- Own your worth.

High self-efficacy correlates with achieving goals, well-being, and problem-solving.

If we want something but it's not happening, we must figure out how to have it. It isn't about that thing being possible or not. It's about figuring out how we can reduce resistance and turn the current in our direction. If there is a limit, it's in us, not out there.

I have been writing consistently since that friendly nudge and using the goal filters: meeting the small goals makes the big more plausible, and it feels better!

Small or big goals. And whatever is happening in your life, now is an excellent time to be brave.

"May the road rise to meet you, May the wind be always at your back ..."

Insight Thirty-Seven:
Stuff That Sticks

Third in a four-part series on Goal Setting and Attainment.

Summary: We reap what we sow.

If you haven't listened to or read the poem from President Biden's Inauguration, I suggest you take a few moments to do so. It's rich with meaning and empowerment for moving forward. Amanda Gorman's Inaugural Poem To me, the phrase that creates a turning point in the message and that we can all embrace in our lives is "And yet the dawn is ours ...."

Also, a helpful note for these times comes from The Shawshank Redemption, "Remember Red, hope is a good thing, maybe the best of things, and no good thing ever dies." Andy Dufresne

When I was in high school in an English class, we got an assignment to take an extensive article and condense it to its essence in a specified number of words. I enjoyed that and got 100% for reducing the text to exactly the target number of words. That experience stuck.

A few years ago, I read Stephen King's book, "On Writing." The most helpful message that sticks with me is the author saying to write just what needs to be said. I think about that too as I write: trying with the least words to say the most.

And I enjoy playful language like alliteration and acronyms like reap and reflect. With reap being an acronym for resistance, enRich, accountability and primer.

Review: Part One was about clarifying a goal or vision and having a wording or empowering structure. Part Two was about shoring up self-efficacy if need be.

A goal with clarity, the "why," worded with empowered structure and fueled with self-efficacy, is like sowing something good. And whatever we sow, we shall reap. To that end, I want to bring some science-based strategies into the field of possibilities to Part Three:

Resistance
- Practice noticing where resistance occurs.
- Fear of success? Fear of failure? Fear of not being perfect?
- Look to evidence to remove unfounded resistance.
- Noticing distractions. Set intentions to overcome.
- Be careful with whom you tell your goals. Avoid naysayers. Seek empowerment in associations.

EnRich (2nd in my program of enVision. enRich. enJoy)

- Most people tend to focus on lack: "I didn't do enough," "I'm not good enough," "I forgot the eggs," "I should have done that better," or "I should have gone further."
- Practice transforming lack thoughts from energy-consuming criticism to energy-creating learning.
- Honour yourself for getting stuff done. Dwell on that which was good and aligned to your desired direction, even if a tiny shift.
- Before sleep, review good facts and bring a sense of feeling good and pride to each little or big accomplishment.
- **Fact:** Repetitive influences change the brain to be more representative of the experiences.

Accountability

- Studies show that accountability reveals a "more likely to achieve the goal" outcome.
- Place yourself in a relationship where you are answerable to someone you respect.
- A Positive Psychology Journal study reveals a **243% higher** score on a group told they would report results to someone versus the other group given the same task but no reporting requirement.
- I gave up watching CNN on a promise to myself I shared with Boyd. And I have a successful agreement with Kerri to call her

at 6:10 each weekday morning for us to write.

- Forms of accountability: (1) Write the goal down (one study showed a **42% increase** in the likelihood of achieving a written goal). (2) Tell a friend. (3) Join or create an accountability group. (4) Hire a coach.

Primers

- Conscious or unconscious cues create a behavioural change.
- One study showed that an unconscious reaction directs 80% of a day's activity based on cues.
- Forms of primers: (1) Post-it signs. (2) Vision board. (3) Music. (4) A particular scent. (5) An inspiring image. (6) A password. (7) Bracelet with meaning. (8) Your unique primer.
- **Study:** Two groups were given a short manual for the task of raising money. The cover of one manual was blank. The other manual had an image of an Olympic runner winning a race. The blank-covered manual group was told to do their best, and the other group got a target. The group with the image and a target raised **283% more** than the first group.

Visualization & Feelings

- A research study showed an **88% correlation** between a real and imagined experience: what we "see" in our mind's

eye matters. Countless studies show
visualization works.

- Feelings are a gateway to more great or
grind. Choose to feel great and experience
more great.

While you wait for the vaccine, here is a potent dose
of gratitude! Gratitude Video - 6 mins

Insight Thirty-Eight:
Excuse Me, I'm Trying to Get Out of My Own Way

Fourth in a four-part series on Goal Setting and Attainment.

Summary: Move forward or around the real or imagined resistance. The view is great when you get through.

Setting a goal and clarifying it in empowering terms (Part One) is the right start to attaining them. If need be, shoring up feelings of self-efficacy (Part Two) provides the belief we can achieve our goals. Understanding areas of resistance, enriching each micro-step along the way liberates our power and creates more, creating accountability, and using primers (Part Three) are ways we can **reap** the good we sow.

It's uphill and feels like a mountain sometimes, but the view is great once we get there!

So, what can slow us down, and is it real or imagined?

Cognitive distortion perfectly describes its meaning, but I'm not too fond of the consequences. There are as many as 15 types of distortions or lies our brain tells us. Here are a few:

- Mental filtering tends to filter out the positives and hold the negatives like a strainer capturing the bad stuff while the good stuff drains away unnoticed.
- Polarized thinking is thinking in extremes, like all or nothing: this rarely being true. We are all imperfect, doing some things very skilfully and some things not.
- Overgeneralization is when not doing well in something once makes us think we are not good at it all the time.
- Personalization is taking things personally: don't; it rarely is.

Cognitive clarity is the opposite of cognitive distortion and the practice of cultivating more truth and positivity:

- Capture and acknowledge the positives and progress by noticing the good facts. Learn from the rest.
- We can moderate our thinking by observing what lies between the extremes and realizing that it represents all of us more accurately.
- We can test generalizing statements or thoughts that feel powerful by asking, "Is this true?"
- People have a lot on their minds. If a friend doesn't text you or call you back, there are all kinds of reasons that could be valid other than being a personal affront.

"The art of being wise is the art of knowing what to overlook." - William James.

It's thought that cognitive distortions are an evolutionary design to keep us safe and survive in short-term stressful situations. But on the other side of safety and survival is the desire to be fully alive by growing into the person we envision through attaining that higher and higher level.

And we can experience a flow state as we attain goals, which is rich evidence that we are wired for growth and expansion because it feels fantastic. Parts of our brain shut down, diverting power to the one focus, which is why often people describe flow as a non-thinking experience.

Flow is a state that can be reached by engaging in a task or goal that is:
- Well defined and at or slightly above our capacity: feeling possible.
- Intrinsically rewarding (doing for the enjoyment of it).
- Free of resistance. With distractions removed, we can get out of our way.

William Murray, in 1951 was on a British reconnaissance team that went to the Everest region to map out a route most likely to get someone to the top on the next trip in 1953. In a book he wrote about the trip, he talks about the power of fully committing to a goal. That famous quote ends with, "Whatever you can do or dream you can begin it. Boldness has genius, power, and magic in it."

If we look at the view ahead and see the horizon and know there is further to go or do or have, we must first honour the distance we have come and all the qualities we possess to have made it this far.

After finishing my 51 km swim across Lake Ontario in a world record time and standing on the shore, still wet and cold, reporters eagerly asked how I felt.

I turned to look back across the lake at the big waves crashing into the break wall and said, "It was hard. I thought about getting out a few times, but glad I didn't." And as I stood there looking at the waves, turbulent water, and dark horizon, I realized that somehow, I had made my way through the waves and cold and unhelpful thoughts and followed up with pride and gratitude by saying, "That was a good swim."

May your little and big inspired goals be empowered by your strength and exceeded by your outcomes.

Insight Thirty-Nine:
Connection Counts

Summary: Doing new things and being a good friend will make each day less like the last.

I was telling my daughters a story of a business trip I once went on to Banff. I had skipped the meetings and skied all day in the magnificent mountains. When the sun went down, I hustled over to a bar where I knew my friends were gathering and leaned into the evening with my first pint.

At the end of the evening, I had gone missing and ended up passed out in a washroom in the Banff Springs Hotel basement. Finally, an RCMP Officer that my friend had enlisted to help found me. I called that friend to tell him I had relived the memory with my daughters. He and I had a blast remembering the trip and vowed to go back with our wives.

It was my birthday on February 01st. I was very grateful several people reached out in various ways to say happy birthday. My mom and siblings called or texted. Friends from different parts of my life, some new and some from when I was a kid, responded on Facebook. I must say that it all felt pretty good.

My daughters made dinner at home, and I put on my colourful Hawaiian shirt and baked a chocolate

165

birthday cake. I slipped some banana slices into the batter to keep them guessing. When taking the pans out of the oven for me, one daughter exclaimed and, inferring dad is a bit weird and we should treat his cooking with caution, said, "what are those chunks?" We had a ton of fun, and I'll remember that evening forever.

And then my brother Dave nudged me to think about connections. We need connections, and friendships are the best kind.

A Harvard Study shows that strong relationships and related social support promote brain health and resilience. Additionally, social connections influence long-term health as much as sleep, diet, and exercise. Dozens of studies show social support helps us be happier, have fewer health issues, and live longer.

Conversely, a lack of social connections links to depression and a shorter life. One study of a lack of social connections increased the risk of premature death by all causes by 50%. That level of risk is higher than obesity and inactivity. Harvard Health

In North America, we celebrate Groundhog Day every February 2nd. The idea is if a groundhog emerges from its burrow and sees its shadow, then winter will persist longer, and if the groundhog doesn't see its shadow, spring will arrive early.

The movie Groundhog Day is a comedy about a news anchor covering the festivities in Punxsutawney, Pennsylvania, who relives that day over and over. The funny people at the movie channel I get played Groundhog Day over and over all day long on the day.

During this COVID lockdown, many people were bored as each day rolled into the next day, much like the last with no clear end in sight.

After some denial, anger, bargaining, and depression, Phil Connors (Bill Murray's character in Groundhog Day) reached acceptance. Maybe this fits today with some of us grieving our loss of a regular life and trips and dinners out and friends we haven't seen for a year or more.

In acceptance, Phil learns to play the piano, becomes an ice sculptor, reads philosophy, learns French, and gets adept at card throwing into a hat. And through all that, he also gets a lot closer to people like the older man he tries to save. It seems all the living he chooses to do and the social connections he fosters were enough to break the spell.

Friendships get created through events that connect us. These novel events are stored in our hippocampus and become memories. As I focused on friendships in the last few weeks, I found that a unique memory was retrieved and relived for each person, bringing many warm smiles to my face.

167

As we might feel the depressive effects of lost connections and days that all feel the same, we can uplift our days by injecting some novelty and being a good friend, which relives and creates new memories that enrich us all.

I'm going to wear my Hawaiian shirt more and crank up my favourite tunes. And do stuff that creates fun memories. Go for a walk where I haven't been before. And be grateful for friendships. Thank you so much for being a friend.

Suggestions:
- Connect with a friend and tell them how much you appreciate them.
- Relive some fun memories. And create new ones.
- Go snowshoeing if you've never been.
- Plan that trip you will take when cleared for "take-off."
- Get dressed for dinner at home and bring out the fine china.
- Have a theme night (we did "Christmas in the Caribbean" when our trip got canceled!)

Let's help each other come out of this ahead.

Here are two books on the importance of friendships. Friendship Matters: How to transform your life ...and Friendship: The evolution, biology and extraordinary power ...

Insight Forty:
Reflections from One to Forty

I thought I would review the last 39 Letters and provide some reflections:

The first insight was, "It's ok to close your eyes." That starting point was about a guy I worked with who gave me heck for closing my eyes at a conference. I knew it would be a very long drive home after a long day. So I just closed my eyes to breathe and focus and rest for a minute or two. It's ok to close your eyes. It's ok to take a break.

From the Third Insight, Neuroplasticity in a "nutshell." What we dwell on and experience changes the brain to create thoughts that support those influences. Given that about 70% of our thoughts are negative, it is critical not to believe and dwell on every thought we have.

"The greatest weapon against stress is our ability to choose one thought over another." - William James.

Insight Four: Life is better if the first thing is for you. I think our job is to do the work that brings us alive. Starting each day, settled and in control, practicing self-direction creates the patterns that support optimizing the route!

Think Roger Federer, walking onto centre court. Control. Leaning in with confident anticipation. Ready to take care of business.

Insight Nine Summary: Rest, fuel, movement, and mindset matter. Do them well for more life. When we thrive, we are on purpose. Our purpose is synonymous with expressing ourselves at the highest possible level, just like any other part of nature.

Insight Ten: Listening - It was just a game. Or was it?
I ran a listening and non-listening exercise with many groups. When not listened to, the response I heard in those sessions that struck me most was people saying they felt like stopping and not saying anything more. This response was typical in every session I did. Imagine the loss of connection and the quiet hurt when someone doesn't listen to you. What was not said? In part, disengagement at work is because people don't feel heard.

Insight Twelve: Mindfulness Part One. The brain changes itself based on the environment and what we dwell on. Therefore, by settling our minds, stress is reduced, we gain a higher level of self-regulation, which supports our human capital's optimization.

Insight Thirteen: Mindfulness – Part Two Awareness. We are not our thoughts. We can practice awareness so we can get some distance

170

and perspective from our thoughts, and be discerning. "Hmm ... I am angry. That's curious." Awareness allows for a pause before a reaction. Unless your house is on fire, a pause is usually a good thing.

Insight Twenty-One: Appreciation. It's a core human need to feel valued and recognized. Evolutionarily it meant survival. People feel seen, heard, valued, and a sense of connection when they are appreciated.

Insight Twenty-Two: Flow. When you move into a state of flow, some natural energy consumers shut down. Our built-in sense of time pauses, and our inner critic quiets right down: all things feel possible, happiness experienced, and performance maximized, the body and mind optimized.

Insight Twenty-five: Manwell. In this insight, I went on a bit of rant, starting with the fact that men die before women at every age. In some countries, men die on average as much as ten years before women. And then into toxic leadership in countries and companies, aggression, and sexual abuse. So my gender needs some work, in some cases, a transformation.

It's good to reflect.

Insight Forty-One:
The Cost Can't be Calculated

If you dropped in from another world and read the headlines, it wouldn't look good for us.

While it's our nature to be attracted to the negative, at a high level, there is evidence that things are trending to be much better in the long game. Why the world is becoming a better place.

But there is still darkness. The other day, I was disgusted to see a news headline about boys' sexual abuse in British Columbia by six Christian Brothers. They had been transferred from the Mount Cashel Orphanage in Newfoundland after abuses in the 1950s.

I listened to a recent BBC Report talking about kids being killed by sniper fire in Yemen, about 450 in the last six years.

Unimaginable horror and human cost.

Monster, an international online employment service, did a study that revealed about 90% of employees say they had been bullied at work, 51% said their boss bullied them, and 39% said co-workers had bullied them. According to the survey, of those who have experienced bullying, 65% left.

A friend of mine, a senior leader, told me she had had the most challenging year of her career due to a bully at work. She confided in a senior peer who said something to the effect of, "well, she has a tough job, you know."

Most employees would prefer their boss be let go to get a raise, while most bosses report they are pretty darn good. There are all kinds of nasty physical and mental health issues that can arise from the effects of bullying—more cost.

During my wealth management career, I have encountered bullies who relished hurting others and bandits who acted unethically and cheated clients. Unfortunately, that ugly aspect of my career experience was like a microcosm of the current political world stage; bullies and bandits are easy to pick out in the media these days.

The full cost of all that madness can't be calculated.

Years ago, there was a kids' show called The Big Comfy Couch. At the end of each episode, the main character looks around the room after all the playing and goings-on and says, "Wait a minute, who made this big mess?" and then she goes on to admit, "Me. I did, didn't I "and "Well I have to clean it up, it's only fair." That began the idea of the "ten-second tidy."
The COVID 19 threat has hit us hard. It has been an urgent global issue like none other in our lifetime. Coincident with this tragedy has been

heightened international cooperation, tolerance, and compassion.

We could argue that at no other time can we remember being all in something together. Not entirely, but more cohesion.

I know the world we have created, the mess, is very complicated.

But what if, like the COVID 19 reaction, we all decided to bring even more awareness to the global challenges and treat them like imminent threats to humankind: areas like Global Health, Food and Water Security, Global Mental Health, Education, Gender Equality, Ocean Health, and Wildlife Preservation. The United Nations has 17 related Goals for 2030 UN Global Goals.

What if we crushed the current COVID 19 threat and got back to life and worked differently? What if we kept that heightened cooperation, tolerance, and compassion and even up-leveled those uniquely human traits to take us to an even better place?

What if we kept all the good that has come from being in this together? And kept building on that? What if we came clean, admitted to the mess, and doubled down on doing even more for the common good? Maybe a "Ten-Year Tidy," which would coincide with the UNs 2030 Goals.

I'm betting the bombs and bullets stores have been open through this pandemic or maybe curbside pick-up. But what if we all decided there is something that matters more. Imagine the degree of global growth and wellbeing that would unfold if we attained the UN Global Goals with humanity at its best instead of attacking each other in little and big ways.

Here is an inspiring story of what is possible with people coming to a vision. Captain Tom Moore just died at age 100. He was the British man who sought a few pledges from friends to walk around his garden in frail health. His goal was to raise 1,000 Pounds Sterling for health care workers. Instead, he ended up raising almost $50 million, with donations coming from 163 countries!

"In the long history of humankind (and animal-kind, too), those who learned to collaborate and improvise most effectively have prevailed." - Charles Darwin.

If we hope for an even better world together, an African proverb helps us,

"When you pray, move your feet."

Insight Forty- two:
What's Love Got to Do with It?

This week and next week, I want to talk about our hearts and love. I found a site with 154 words with "heart" in it, like hearty, hearten, heartbreak, heartache, and sweetheart. But maybe our heart is just a pump? A pretty stunning, best-in-class pump.

At six weeks, when a fetus is about the size of a grain of rice, the heart begins to beat. So we were once the size of a grain of rice with a heart that magically just started to beat.

I take a lot of my bodily functioning for granted and feel I would not do well on an anatomy test asking where things are and how they work. As for the heart, the right side of the heart draws blood from our veins. This blood coming from the body to the heart is low in oxygen and is pumped to the lungs to drop off carbon dioxide and pick up more oxygen.

Our lungs move oxygen to the left side of the heart, which pumps it through arteries to the rest of the body. And on and on. Every heartbeat moves about one-third of a cup of blood through our system. Our hearts beat between 60 and 100 times per minute. At 60 bpm, that's about 28,700 cups of blood or 1,800 gallons each day cycling through our body. Suppose you imagine your SUV or the one next to you at the gas station filling up. The gas tank of an average SUV is about 40 gallons. So our bodies circulate about 45 SUV tanks worth of blood every day.

You could stop for a moment, close your eyes and feel or listen to your heart beating and give thanks for such a precious, efficient piece of internal hardware. Maybe once in a while, we should put a hand over our heart in a quiet moment and say thank you.

But where is our heart? Our heart is more to the centre of our chest than we might think; about two-thirds of it is left of centre and one-third to the right of centre.

Cardiovascular disease or CVDs are disorders of the heart and blood vessels that collectively are the number one cause of death globally. *Source: The World Health Organization*

The good news is that 80% of CVD is preventable by caring for our heart, the most efficient, reliable pump there is. And here is what the pump needs from us:
- Adequate exercise.
- A healthy diet.
- Proper sleep.
- Managed stress.

Harvard Heart Health

The mind and body are connected: our thoughts influence how we feel. For example, a relaxed mind calms the body and lowers our heart rate by activating the parasympathetic nervous system. Conversely, a busy, stressed mind activates the

177

sympathetic nervous system, increases our heart rate, and prepares us to fight or flee. Well designed to handle a short burst of stress, low-level chronic activation is hard on our hearts.

There is a lot of literature about the connection between our heart and love. My sense of it is this: We know that the amygdala is the source of emotional memory and activation for an immediate reaction like fighting or fleeing. An emotional response is about an aversion to something, a rush to conflict, or getting away quickly from potential harm. And all of that is immediately felt in the body as a real threat. And if prolonged, it will be very unhealthy.

I think love is a similar mechanism of stimulation but triggers the opposite. Instead of a threat, we feel safety and connection, and all that is very compelling, sometimes euphoric.

Love comes in many forms and grades. First love. Love of a spouse or a child. Love of a sport or love for being in nature or art. Love for ourselves. Love in all its forms is uplifting and healthy (happier, less anxiety, stress, and helps us live longer).
I wonder, could love apply at work? It's not quite in the way you just imagined, but love for another human being that we can realize is more alike than different, challenged just like we are from time to time. In this context, maybe love is more comfortable to hear as compassion which has the

same health consequences as love (without the trip to HR!).

Since work accounts for about 75% of our lives' stress, more compassionate leadership and environments would be better. By the way, that isn't soft stuff; that is an ingredient of healthy high performance in teams and optimized human capital.

When my daughters were young, I would tell them that love is the most powerful force in the universe. Then, of course, they would say I was wrong that gravity is the most powerful force. I'm sticking with love, but it's very much like gravity!

Tina Turner sang, "What's love got to do with it? Maybe the answer depends on what "it" is?

If "it" is living a rich, fulfilling, resilient long life together, maybe the answer is "everything."

Insight Forty-Three:
The Second Of Two Insights on Our
Heart and Love. A Good Heart Stopped
and What Einstein Didn't Say.

I once read an astute observation about life: time and attention are the only two things we have.

We have an unknown amount of time. And choices all day long as to what to give our attention. So it seems we could think about net attention benefit, as the difference between attention to "junkie" or "juicy" things, the net of attention that uplifts us, others we care about, and the life we live together.

Milo was a guy in his mid-fifties who I observed often showed up early to the masters' swim workout and stayed when others had hit the showers. All, to get more good work in. I admired that. He didn't settle for doing it the way most others did it.

When I saw him at the Club, he was always engaged, enthusiastic and encouraged me to come for a swim. He always seemed self-directed to the goal of making the best use of time and attention.
Tragically and sadly, he died of a heart attack about ten days ago. I didn't know him that well, but his dedication and hard work inspired me, and I'm going to hold onto my admiration of his focus and how he paid attention well in the time he had.

180

When my daughters were young, I would tell them that love is the most powerful force there is. But, of course, they would say I am wrong. Gravity, they say, is the most powerful force in the universe. So, I was only too happy to find this letter from Einstein to one of his daughters to confirm my belief!

In the late 1980s, Lieserl, the daughter of the famous genius, donated 1,400 letters, written by Einstein, to the Hebrew University, with orders not to publish their contents until two decades after his death. This is one of the letters for Lieserl Einstein.

"When I proposed the theory of relativity, very few understood me, and what I will reveal now to transmit to mankind will also collide with the misunderstanding and prejudice in the world I ask you to guard the letters as long as necessary, years, decades, until society is advanced enough to accept what I will explain below.

There is an extremely powerful force that, so far, science has not found a formal explanation to. It is a force that includes and governs all others, and is even behind any phenomenon operating in the universe and has not yet been identified by us. This universal force is LOVE. When scientists looked for a unified theory of the universe, they forgot the most powerful unseen force. Love is Light that enlightens those who give and receive it. Love is gravity, because it makes some people feel attracted to others. Love is power, because it multiplies the best we have, and allows humanity not to be extinguished in their blind selfishness. Love unfolds and reveals. For love we live and die. Love is God and God is Love.

This force explains everything and gives meaning to life. This is the variable that we have ignored for too long, maybe because we are afraid of love because it is the only energy in the universe that man has not learned to drive at will. To give visibility to love, I made a simple substitution in my most famous equation. If instead of E = mc2, we accept that the energy to heal the world can be obtained through love multiplied by the speed of Light squared, we arrive at the conclusion that love is the most powerful force there is, because it has no limits. After the failure of humanity in the use and control of the other forces of the universe that have turned against us, it is urgent that we nourish ourselves with another kind of energy.

If we want our species to survive, if we are to find meaning in life, if we want to save the world and every sentient being that inhabits it, love is the one and only answer. Perhaps we are not yet ready to make a bomb of love, a device powerful enough to entirely destroy the hate, selfishness and greed that devastate the planet. However, each individual carries within them a small but powerful generator of love whose energy is waiting to be released. When we learn to give and receive this universal energy, dear Lieserl, we will have affirmed that love conquers all, is able to transcend everything and anything, because love is the quintessence of life.

I deeply regret not having been able to express what is in my heart, which has quietly beaten for you all my life. Maybe it's too late to apologize, but as time is relative, I need to tell you that I love you and thanks to you I have reached the ultimate answer!"

Your father, Albert Einstein

There is debate about the author of the letter. One legitimate-looking source I reviewed claims for a variety of reasons Einstein did not write it. Einstein's Letter to a Daughter

Still, I think the message is worthy of our attention. Love is given and received and "multiplied by the speed of light squared." Yup. Sounds about right. Awesomely powerful!

Limited time. Unknown expiry date. Let's make it as "juicy" as possible.

Insight Forty-Four:
The F Word. It's Not What You Think

When I was Managing an office in the wealth management business, I met an adult child of an elderly client who had just passed away. We needed a few legal documents to satisfy the legal department to move the money to her as a beneficiary. It became evident that the other child of the deceased was not sharing in the financial assets, and that sibling was now objecting to the Will.

Then this person said something that struck me, "My sister hurt my mom, and there is no way I will let her have any of this money, and I will use every last penny of this inheritance if I have to make sure she doesn't get any."

Sometimes we choose to hold on to the hurt or harm we feel, even if done to another person. The crazy thing is if we hold the hurt, we continue to be the victim. We can allow the hurt and harm to hold our heart and mind hostage. Then, for a bit of time or a lifetime, we could feel it's legitimate not to forgive.

We might feel offended, hurt, made to feel unheard, harmed, or treated unjustly by someone or a company. There are some pretty good reasons for being hurt. We might be so offended that our sense of pride or values was so disrespected that we will dig in as if waiting for some tribunal to validate us.

"Don't carry a grudge. While you are carrying the grudge, the other guy's out dancing.". Buddy Hacket

Not forgiving can consume a lot of energy and turn out to tear away at our vitality like a second-level offense, but this time self-imposed.

"Unforgiveness is stressful, and holding unforgiving emotions and motives for long periods can take a toll on our bodies, leading to elevated blood pressure, heart rate, or cortisol. If those elevations persist, they can cause stress-related problems (i.e., mental health problems and problems like elevated cardiovascular)." Source: The Science of Forgiveness, Everett Worthington Jr.

We might have felt the company itself hurt us. But what is more logical is that the company made a decision that hurt. And maybe the decision that hurt wasn't handled skillfully. Our hearts and values are so precious that we might be expecting everyone to be perfect at respecting us. That is a lot to ask. We can take it all personally, and often it isn't.

If we consider forgiveness, it doesn't mean we condone the behaviour or what happened was okay. Instead, it means we can free ourselves from the unhealthy bond we have kept alive with the offender or event.

Why consider forgiving:
We might not have the whole story.
What has been the cost of holding the hurt, and what will be the future cost?
What if we are wrong and there was no intended offense?
Forgiveness is a release and frees up energy.
Maybe someone has forgiven us, and we see room to forgive.

"Studies have found that the act of forgiveness can reap huge rewards for your health, lowering the risk of a heart attack; improving cholesterol levels and sleep; and reducing pain, blood pressure, and levels of anxiety, depression, and stress. And research points to an increase in the forgiveness-health connection as you age." Source: John Hopkins Medicine

Notice that the health consequences to the person hurt are almost precisely the opposite of unforgiving to forgiving.

Easy to say. A heroic effort sometimes to forgive.

You might consider reflecting on these forgiveness statements in a quiet moment:
If I have hurt or harmed anyone, knowingly or unknowingly, I ask for forgiveness.
If anyone has hurt or harmed me, knowingly or unknowingly, I forgive them.

And we all know the forgiveness opportunity applies to us too.
For all the ways I have hurt or harmed myself knowingly or unknowingly, I offer forgiveness.

Choose very carefully who and what we allow to live and settle in our minds.

Resource: Jack Kornfield: A powerful message of forgiveness

Insight Forty-five:
Correlation – Can't Escape The
"Numbers"

_____

Below is the formula for correlation.

> The correlation coefficient, r, is the measure of strength of the relationship or association between two things: r can range from −1.00 (negative) to +1.00 (positive). An r of 0 indicates no correlation such as between drinking tea and intelligence.

$$r = \frac{n(\Sigma xy) - (\Sigma x)(\Sigma y)}{\sqrt{[\,n\Sigma x^2 - (\Sigma x)^2\,][\,n\Sigma y^2 - (\Sigma y)^2\,]}}$$

Even though this isn't a math class, we know the outcomes don't lie.

David was an advisor in a wealth management office of which I was Branch Manager. He did something wrong. He crossed the regulatory line, and I had to fine him. Perfect negative correlation:

"if you do the crime, you have to do time." He didn't accept the correlation as clearly as I did.

Priding myself on a respectful communication style and fair treatment policy, I thought the meeting in my office would be pretty straightforward. I said, "David, you can pay the fine in one lump sum, or we can take it off your pay in installments." At that, he started yelling at me and threatened to have his lawyer charge me with theft and have the police come and take me away. I lashed out. Then he leaned forward with a softer but more aggressive tone and told me he would have me fired and removed as Branch Manager. At this point, I stood up, towering over him, and continued yelling at him.

Thankfully, an arising voice of sanity in my mind got through the madness, and to avoid a further escalation, I ended the meeting.

One of my brothers was struggling with career direction, and seeing such potential and a variety of options for him, I had dished out lots of well-intentioned advice, like, "you should do this." or "why don't you do that?" Or, "if you did this, it would be huge."

From my barrage of "support," I thought something would stick and help like + 1 of association between advice and take up. However, on most calls, there was silence at the end of the line.

The lack of engagement made sense as I reflected on our declining relationship on my walk home one night because I was doing most of the talking and a lot of the words came across as judgment.

The illusion of judgment is that it's a quick fix: "you are doing it wrong," "I can see a better way," and here it is all laid out.

It dawned on me on that walk home years ago that my messages, while intending to be helpful, weren't but instead causing a negative correlation in our relationship, a -1: a negative message and negative response.

I walked a few more steps in thought and stopped asking myself, "What if I just love him?" From that step forward, I tried my best to come from a place of love and compassion and listen better. The correlation curve shifted, albeit slowly, to a better trajectory, solidly in positive territory now.

It matters significantly to outcomes just how we speak and act in our lives. For example, is there a consciously constructed message or action with good odds of a good result? Or is the communication unconsciously driven, hoping that the other person will somehow get the message right but likely won't.

Being sad isn't going to make us happy. Being mean isn't a successful strategy. Being mad at someone isn't going to bring us closer. From the seed of self-criticism can come learning if we choose it to be, but if not it can
190

disconnect us from that voice in our hearts we feel called to express.

In a study a few years ago, 77% of leaders said they do a good job of engaging with their people, yet 88% of employees say their leaders do a bad job with engagement, and 65% of employees would forgo a pay raise to see their leaders fired.

We can expect a positive correlation between wellness and longevity if we are pretty good at rest, fuel, movement, and mindset. In addition, doing things we love to do is positively correlated to life satisfaction, which is contagious.

But nobody has a perfect positive correlation of +1 between intentions and outcomes, like a straight diagonal line from the "bottom left to the top right" and beyond. That would be nice.

In real life, it's a choppy line from day-to-day expected positive correlations of things we say or do and outcomes that are different from the plan. But, on balance, the curve can be upward trending. Learning is fuel for an optimal trajectory. And the degree to which we learn, can be aware, conscious, intentional, and compassionate to ourselves and others, that life curve line will look better and better

Insight Forty-Six:
There Can Be Ties for First

A good friend sent me a note suggesting I write about "Putting me first" with the idea that we can easily look after others in our lives and, in so doing, find ourselves at the bottom of the list.

The topic resonated. Once I was lousy at self-care; now, I am better at it. But then I wondered if the issue is so widespread that low-level self-care is just accepted as the way to operate. And an argument suggesting we could look after ourselves well might be met with, "sounds good but no time for me" or "I have a lot of responsibilities, and they come first." So then I began to re-think what I would write about this week, if not self-care.

Two of my daughters happened to be in the kitchen last night, so I explained my dilemma of not knowing what to say. I asked them, "why do you think people generally are not good at looking after themselves and much better at looking after others?" One answer came quickly, "primal instinct." Evolutionarily it makes sense to be wired to look after others to be of value and survive in groups.

Then came, "people think self-care is selfish, but it isn't," and then finally, "we are taught that it's better to look after others first and selfish or wrong to look after ourselves first." I asked if they felt I had taught them that. "No," they said. "Society has."

I took some responsibility and reminded them of my days of madness when they were little, caused by my low level of self-care. I have apologized to my girls for things said and done during that crazy period.

There are consequences of a trajectory of low self-care.

Years ago, a relative in his 70s was dying. I went to visit him in the hospital. As if to reconcile his state or maybe as a warning, he looked at me and said, "I just didn't look after myself."

I went online and searched why we are better at looking after others than ourselves. Here are a few insights worthy of considering:
- Self-care goes against the masculine or tough-guy role of the expectation of handling it all.
- Competition in a "pressure to perform" world may make self-care seem like a luxury.
- Identity one holds of themselves can be highly attached to work which restricts perspective.
- Not raised with a healthy role model.
- The "must provide for" model may exclude self-care.

- Life is just too busy and complex to have time for me.
- Learned unimportance of needs could come from childhood.
- A low sense of deserving (low self-esteem or self-worth).

Why Men Suck at Self Care

We tend to think in terms of priorities, one thing being more important than another. A typical interview question would be how one deals with conflicting priorities. We think of importance in a vertical list, from 1 to 10. In the context of doing for others, it's easy to make a list like:

1. Spouse
2. Kids
3. Parents
4. Siblings
5. Work responsibilities
6. Money
7. Walking the dogs

In a show, my kids like to watch a character proposed marriage to his girlfriend, saying, "I love you, and I am prepared to put you ahead of me for the rest of my life." I get the pitch, but I don't think that's a good formula for success.

I woke up years ago to realize the effort required to maintain a mindset of being the best husband, best dad, the best son, and the best Manager at work was the primary cause of my declining health. I realized that being last or feeling last created a contraction in the enjoyment of life. But having a few equal top areas of importance, me being one, supported an expansion of health and happiness.

Maybe the answer to that interview question is, "while I take care of myself, I can do my best to address the urgency and importance of other priorities."

I came across this prayer of compassion that I read regularly:
- I am generating and extending compassion for all living beings.
- May all living beings be happy and free from suffering.
- I offer my happiness and good qualities to all living beings.
- I cherish all living beings.

Honestly and uncomfortably, it felt like the last bit was for others only.

To make it feel right, I added "including myself" to the last line.

Be well too,

Insight Forty-Seven:
Our Mind Has the Answers. Just Ask

Each week when I think about writing these Insights, I ask myself, "what do I want to say this week?" Then I listen closely. The other day I asked that question, and what dropped in was "questions." Then I asked, "what is it that I want to say about questions?" The answer came "that asking a question helps."

This brain of ours contains 86 billion brain cells or neurons, and each one is connected to thousands of other neurons. It's estimated that we have hundreds of trillions of neuronal connections resulting in massive connectivity.

Stored in these trillions of connections are every experience we have had, every bit of learning, the ability to create an infinite number of possible scenarios, unleashing unbounded creativity, and is devoted to our most aspired self. And this "algorithm" holds every evolutionary success trait since life began about 3.5 billion years ago.

You could ask it any question you like, anytime and as many times as you like. But in our private world of self-talk, do we make statements or ask questions?

A core element of psychology is how our thoughts determine how we feel, which means how we predominantly think determines how we predominantly feel.

"Why should we think upon things that are lovely? Because thinking determines life. It is a common habit to blame life upon the environment. Environment modifies life but does not govern life. The soul is stronger than its surroundings." William James

I think the "algorithm" wants to supply the best answer to move us forward, to thrive, which is what evolution is all about. Sometimes we make statements that might be great if they are affirmative or deserving, like, "I am smart" or "I am good enough," Or not so ok if we dwell on distorted thoughts: no amount of those will make us feel good.

Sometimes the things we think are simply not true, and our self-evaluation merely lies. While self-criticism can be good if we learn and turn it into good, much of it seems to keep us stalled or stuck. And statements, like "I don't know," "I'm not sure," "I don't like this," or "I don't feel motivated," or "I feel overwhelmed" don't activate the mind to solutions and can make us feel flat and uninspired.

We somehow think these thoughts will solve the problem but aren't helpful.

To ask questions of ourselves is a whole other story. Good questions activate the mind to generate ideas and answers. And a rested mind is even more friendly to high-quality solutions.

Benefits of asking ourselves questions:
- Shifting from feeling stuck to unstuck.
- Relief and renewed forward motion can occur.
- Creating options when it might not have seemed there were any.
- Supporting self-efficacy and capacity.
- Give a broader perspective.
- Asking big questions could change a life or the world.

A celebrated American poet, Mary Oliver, wrote, *"Tell me, what is it you plan to do with your one wild and precious life?"*

A few other good questions to ask are:
- What makes me happy?
- What do I most value?
- What do I want?
- What do I need to feel better?
- Who could help me?
- Is there a better way?
- Does this serve me?
- How do I feel right now?
- What one thing can I do to feel better?
- Is that thought true?
- How am I showing up, and is that how I want to show up?

- How do I want to treat myself today?
- What do I want to accomplish today?
- What actions will it take to achieve this?

Ask.
Listen closely.
Take good notes.

Insight Forty-Eight:
What Becomes Before Matters to What Comes After

An te ced ent
- Adjective: preceding; prior to; an antecedent event.

We have two red labs, and the youngest is Chili. She is exuberant. She is also small for a lab but lives large and has an inspiring outlook: every dog and every person a potential friend.

Her training has been slow in taking effect due to her outlook and my sometimes frustration with it. However, a great dog trainer has helped us realize that what is going on is really human training: optimally communicating through patterns, commands, and presence.

A few months ago, I let Chili off her leash in the corner of a small park near where we live because she wanted to play with another dog. Then that dog ran to the opposite corner of the park where a child I had seen earlier was playing. Chili is at high speed, chasing the dog, oblivious to my "stop" command.

I got nervous about upsetting the child and mother and tried to get a hold of my dog. Chili was having a blast, and the LAST thing she was interested in

200

was me and the leash. Finally, I got her under control and was mad because she wouldn't do what I said and because I let her off and should have projected that risk.

I related my frustration to our dog trainer, who I like to call Coach. She came back with some wisdom she heard at a virtual dog training conference that "almost all training problems are antecedent problems."

My take on that was what comes before matters to what comes after.

I have a great pair of hiking boots. They took me up and down Mount Kenya and Mount Kilimanjaro and through lots of local hikes. The boots are old. The laces are new and long enough for eight eyelets on each side. Last weekend I was rushing to put them on. I laced up one boot. Then unknowingly was standing on the other boot's lace, trying to take a step forward against the resistance of the lace I was standing on.

Sometimes I will turn the water on in the kitchen sink only to find someone had left a teaspoon right side up, directly under the faucet. When the water hits the spoon's concave surface at full speed, it splashes out everywhere. The placing of the spoon in the sink is antecedent to the spray and my annoyance.

The other thing our human training Coach passed along is that part of the learning is "how to set up the dog better to succeed." And if we set up the environment so that the dog can succeed, we don't get into scenarios where the dog is running around unmanageably.

Then there is the pothole story. A guy walks along a street and steps right into a large deep pothole. He is bewildered and has a hard time getting out, so he needs help. The next day he walks along the same street and falls into the same hole again. He gets out himself. On the third day, he walks along, sees the hole but still falls in. On the fourth day, he sees the hole and walks around it. On the fifth day, he takes a different route.

Sometimes we keep doing the same thing and wondering why the outcome isn't different from last time. Does anything come up for you? Is there an outcome you would prefer that will require a shift in its antecedent behaviour?

Considerations
- Practice bringing attention to what has caused the unintended outcome in the past.
- Accept it as fact in a way that allows for freedom to change and make a new choice.
- Be intentional about your desired outcome.
- Consider what makes up the best setup of your environment for the success of the intended result.

Strategies

- A self-supporting morning routine: Sit quietly, breathe, uplifting reading, make notes in your journal, set intentions for the day.
- Eat a healthy breakfast.
- Become ok with closing your eyes and taking a few deep breaths and long exhales during the day for a micro-rest.
- Move around (exercise).
- Ask yourself good questions about what you need to complete tasks and challenges successfully.
- Dwell on good facts from your day.
- Prioritize sleep.

Chili and I are doing much better. My ease and better judgment seem to help her be at ease and more in control. I will make sure my boot laces are free and clear the next time I get ready for a hike. I now look in the sink first before turning on the tap.

Let's watch out for "potholes" in our path and mindfully make what comes before better, so what comes after is best.

Insight Forty-Nine:
Magic

Years ago, I was walking one of my daughters home from school. She seemed to be thinking hard and turned to me and said, "Dad, are fairies for real life?" I thought about that for a few seconds and replied, "Yes, my love. Fairies are magic, and magic is real."

*"Children see magic because they look for it. "*Christopher Moore.

Most of what I write about are the observations from a growing awareness that became more activated when I awoke from a great deal of stress and decided to do my life differently: going from madness to magic.

One searing memory of being deep in the madness of chronic stress was an evening when I was trying to get one of my daughters to bed. She "wasn't tired," and I got furious. In reflection, I was so far away from a clear mind that I couldn't see the magic that was right in front of me.

The way back was through an intention for change.

"Waking up" to the laser clear thought that there must be a different way to do my life set the intention for a better way.

204

For me, the road back was attending to my sleep, diet, exercise, and my mindset; the first three were foundational requirements to a healthier mind. And part of my brain hygiene work was beginning a regular mindfulness meditation practice: this changed many things for the good.

At work, I experienced less stress, more focus, improved relationships, and more effective leadership. At some point, I read a great book by Maria Gonzalez called Mindful Leadership. I sent her an email to say how the book helped me. As a result, I experienced more rich collaborative outcomes in being more mindful and present in leadership, and I intended to develop myself in this area further.

Maria wrote back and said, "When we set intentions, significant changes start to take shape. Soon you will find that mindfulness will get imbued in everything you do, every presentation, every client meeting, every conversation, every meal, every drive home. That then becomes a figure-ground reversal."

I didn't know what figure-ground reversal meant, so I looked it up and took it to mean refined "vision," more awareness, seeing differently what otherwise was unnoticed.
"Didn't see it at all. Now I see it everywhere." - Olivia Crane.

The more common experience of figure-ground reversal is the picture of the young lady who transforms into an old lady or, here, the image of the vase, or is it a picture of two faces?

There is a changing visual relationship between the "figure" in the foreground and the "ground" in the background. The "reversal" happens when we see something that wasn't there before in our field of vision.

"There are two ways to live your life. One is as though nothing is a miracle. The other is as though everything is a miracle." Albert Einstein

I think figure-ground reversal is a fancy term for magic: seeing or experiencing something that was there all along but has now come into the light of our perception.

"Miracles happen every day: change your perception of what a miracle is, and you'll see them all around you." Jon Bon Jovi

I was struck recently by a song by the Doobie Brothers called "Listen to the Music." We could think of music like magic. Both come from an endless source of creation; both inspire and give us a sense of hope. I felt that the lyrics play well into the current challenges we are all experiencing.

Don't you feel it growing day by day?
People gettin' ready for the news.
Some are happy, some are sad
Oh ... we got to let the music play.
Whoa, oh whoa,
Listen to the Music.
Whoa, oh whoa,
Listen to the Music

What we pay attention to grows day by day in our minds. These are super challenging times, and we can be primed and ready for the news each day through which we can see a lot of the sadness, but no amount of sadness is the vaccine.

In addition to getting the "jab," we can acknowledge the challenges and then support ourselves to be intentional about what we want to see and experience. Then, in the refined vision, we can see more magic!

Suggestions:
- Build a playlist of music you can put on or crank up to move you because despite the challenges, "we got to let the music play."

- Jot down daily or at least weekly the magical things you see and experience: dwell in the good.

Sometimes we just need a little magic!

Insight Fifty:
Blood, It's in Us To Live

It was time for my annual check-up, so I contacted my family doctor. He arranged a blood test as the best measure to gauge my health. That happened pretty quickly, and I got an email message after he had seen the results saying, "your blood work, including cholesterol and PSA, look great."

"Great" sounded good, but I wanted more, so I contacted my naturopath, and we booked a meeting to go through the results in more detail. The report was three and a bit pages: three columns, the test, the results, and the range.

After retrieving the report and printing it off the day before the meeting, I looked down the list of tests and flipped the pages thinking, "holy shit, a lot is going on in my blood!" WBC, RBC, Hemoglobin, Hematocrit, MCV, MCH, RDW, Platelet count, and that was just the first ¼ of the first page! And I don't want to forget the Glomerular Filtration Rate and the Alanine Aminotransferase on page two.

Later I was out for a walk and met a friend who has a dog that loves to play with my dog. He mentioned a co-worker who has a severe thyroid issue that allowed an infection to get out of control, and she is in a serious condition because of it.

Taking that story in and with the pages of lab results in my mind, I became overwhelmed. I know about some stuff that goes on inside, but I don't understand all of it, like the implications of a slightly high Thyroid Stimulating Hormone (TSH) in my blood.

My naturopath is enthusiastic. When we hit an hour, I had to remind her of the time, or we would have just kept going. We ended up with seven measurements that needed a slight nudge up or down to move to more optimal. We set up another blood test in three months to see what would have changed.

Life travels in the blood.

How we do our life like the four cornerstone domains of sleep, diet, activity level, and thinking (stress & mindset) directly show up in our blood, like a scorecard with no secrets but consequences. No sustained impairment of one of the four domains will go unnoticed on the inside, while the outside may look fine.

Depletion shows up in our blood. And a deficit can't reveal our highest aspiration.

Conversely, life is sustained and optimized when we rest well, fuel ourselves properly, move around, and create a healthy mindset. Wellness travels in the blood.

For our blood to maintain and extend us, there is a formula.

My mother is 93 ½, lives on her own, can't see well now, but still is a force of nature. The other day I spent some time with her and asked her if she had any ideas of what I should write about this week. Without hesitation, she quickly said, "gratitude, write about gratitude."

As I listened for more of her wisdom, she seemed to reveal in her comments a formula for the longevity and wellness she enjoys. So here are my notes from that conversation:

Gratitude
- Be grateful for your assets; this underlines the importance of knowing what they are!

Moderation
- Don't overdo it.
- If muscles hurt, pay attention to that.
- Pay attention to what your body is telling you.
- Not paying attention to what we need makes us cranky, tired, and mad.

Prioritize
- Don't do something first that is way down the list.
- Do what is important.

Reasonableness

- If you want to walk a long distance, you have to build up to it.
- Overdoing it, being unreasonable, risks the erosion of our assets.
- Treat your life with reasonableness; otherwise, suffer undue wear and tear.
- Prioritize your own time.

A blood test is like a scorecard derived from how we do our life. The magical thing is that the scorecard has been written in "pencil" and can be adjusted better.

Insight Fifty-One
Letter to Teens

It's tough for many of you. It shouldn't be this hard, and nobody wishes it to be so. And with current COVID lockdowns, it's even more challenging.

The challenges you are experiencing are transforming into record rates of mental distress. The World Health Organization (WHO) knows how hard and important this is:

- Adolescents (10 to 19) represent 1/6th of the world population.
- Half of all mental health issues start by age 14.
- Depression is one of the leading causes of illness and disability among adolescents.
- Suicide is the third leading cause of death in 15-19-year-olds.

Source: The WHO's Global Accelerated Action for Adolescent Health Program AA-AH!

If you find yourself in a state of mental distress, while you may feel alone, I hope you can know you aren't.

I think you guys are growing up too fast and having trouble with the pace. Another way I could say this is an inherent pressure in the speed at which society and technology raise expectations. Including the anxiety, some feel from comparing

213

looks and lifestyles through social media that is outpacing your ability to adapt.

When you entered grade school, the teacher on most days said, "now students open your textbooks" to learn about the outside world and how to read, do the math and write. So I'm curious if you might have felt a bit like, "Hey, I'm feeling a lot of stress here, I want to feel like I can handle it, but it's scary," and then wondering where the textbook is for the inside stuff?

I asked my daughter a few years ago about stress in teens. She turned to me with an odd look and said, "every one of my friends is stressed out. There is too much homework, and if we don't get our homework done, we won't do well on tests, and if we don't get good marks, we won't get into the right school and then won't get the right job."

I know a guy whose wife works as a counselor at a girls' private school, and he told me once about 80% of the kids who seek out his wife are about performance anxiety, like, "I got 85% in math, and I am freaking out."

Another of my daughters told me she feels society expects us to place more importance on looking after others than ourselves.
We can only sustain a healthy effort in big aspirations by taking good care of our minds and body.

214

If you and your buddies were watching a bunch of younger kids in a playground (pre or post COVID!), and someone said, "which of these kids deserves to be happy and healthy?' You undoubtedly would think that was a dumb question because you would say every kid should be on the list.

A friend relates a story of being at a mental health clinic with a daughter. After a bit of chit-chat, the doctor turned to the girl and said, "so, why are you here?" The teenager responded, "because I haven't been myself lately." I hear that comment as a profoundly accurate statement of distress: the body's language announces the gap between how we feel and how we want to feel.

A spiral is cool.

I imagine the centre or starting point could be that birthright of health and happiness, laughing, playing, feeling at ease, lightness, high aspirations, all good stuff. But maybe some self-criticism creeps in, unworthiness, not being enough of something or other.

The more we follow negative thoughts, the more we move around the spiral away from the centre until we say, "how did I get here?"

Like a nasty board game, the further away from the centre, the worse we feel. Sometimes we might feel so far away that we think there is no way back.

But there are many times when we shoot right back to joy as if we pulled a special card and get to take one or two steps through a magic passageway right to the centre instead of going back around the long way.

The trick to pulling that magic card is looking for a reason to feel good, grabbing hold of a happy thought and another and another until, BOOM, you are back to yourself.

That noticing where your thoughts have taken you is like exercise; the more you practice, the better you get. I also know that sometimes searching for a happy thought is very hard.

The thing is, you are SO important—a super precious person. Your parents will never ever look upon another thing they will view as more special and important than you.

In the textbook, there is stuff like:
- Sleeping well matters. You know this because you feel lousy when you don't get a good night's sleep and look great when you do.

- Hate to remind us all, sugar is not good for us: what we choose to put inside us matters.
- If a bedroom becomes a default space to do school, watch movies and avoid parents, it's not likely to feel good for long.
- The outdoors makes us feel better.
- Exercise, even going for a walk, is proven to make us feel better.
- And our minds: they can hurt or help us. Try turning your inner voice to be as if you were speaking to your best friend!

Insight Fifty-Two:
Nature and Wellbeing

Recently I contributed my thoughts to an initiative to protect about 200 acres of land northwest of Toronto in a wellness community. A formidable group is pitching the local County to preserve nature from over development and consider a project aligned to well-being. I wrote two pieces for the submission, (1) the connection between nature and well-being and (2) a concept piece for a global wellness centre.

Well-being can be described as a state of good health, happiness, fulfillment, and purpose, judging one's life positively and feeling engaged in life.

But do we need to look to science to investigate the positive connection between nature and enhanced well-being?

We are nature. Not separate. We know this intuitively because when we experience nature, our breathing slows, deep breaths and long exhales are more effortless; we feel a sense of calm and connection. Likewise, we are reminded of nature's beneficial influence when we see others in nature experience more aliveness, playfulness, and joy, particularly in children.
Being in nature enlivens us. More human. Like coming home. Relief. Restorative.

Florence Williams wrote a book called "The Nature Fix": Why nature makes us happier, healthier, and more creative. The Nature Fix 1:41 Video. Her findings from being in nature:

- Our heart rate slows.
- Our facial muscles relax.
- Our brain's frontal lobe quiets, allowing more creativity and productivity.
- Our immune system works better.
- Calm and alertness are more accessible.
- We enjoy a heightened connection to people and the world around us. (Another study revealed a drop in crime rates by being in nature).

In an article called "How, Immersion in Nature Benefits your Health," Gretchen Daily, the Director of the Natural Capital Project at Stanford University, says, "There is an awakening underway today to many of the values of nature and the risks and costs of its loss." Source: Nature Benefits Health

In 2005 Richard Louv wrote "The Child in the Woods" and was credited with coining "Nature Deficit Disorder." At that time, he could find about 60 studies about the effects of less exposure to nature. By 2020, there were 1,000 studies. Mr. Louv states that all these studies point in one direction, "Nature is not only nice to have, but it's a have-to-have for physical health and cognitive functioning."

219

The three top Consensus Statements from a study by the American Association of the Advancement of Science (AAAS)
1. Evidence supports an association between common types of nature experience and increased psychological well-being.
2. Evidence supports an association between common types of nature experiences and a reduction of risk factors and the burden of some types of mental illness.
3. Evidence suggests that opportunities for some types of nature experience have decreased in quantity and quality for many people worldwide.
Source: Nature and Mental Health

Doctors in Europe and 34 US States are now prescribing nature to their patients. And this recent article about PaRx (Park Prescriptions) follows suit. Ontario Doctors prescribe nature to ailing patients. Some brief points:
- The UK Wildlife Trust: "almost a 700% return on every pound sterling invested in connecting people with nature."
- A 2014 survey showed Canadians spent about 94% of their time inside or in a car.
- A 2020 Canadian survey showed that 70 percent of respondents had an increased appreciation for parks and green spaces, 82 percent view parks as important to their mental health, and 70 percent to their physical health.
- About 75% of all disease is preventable. The U.S. Centers for Disease Control and

Prevention reports, "enhanced park use and physical activity sufficient to achieve just a five-per-cent reduction in the burden of diabetes, hypertension, and related conditions could save an estimated $24.7 billion annually in avoided health-care costs."

Science then becomes of value in making a case for the economic and social "Return on Nature." Embedded in these attributes of being in nature are more optimized human capital and reduced health care costs: the respective increase and decrease leveraging better communities and world.

"In every walk with nature, one receives far more than he seeks." - John Muir

Go outside more. Life is better that way.

Insight Fifty-Three:
Reminder, it's Ok to Close Your Eyes

Insight One sent out a year ago was entitled, "It's ok to close your eyes." It was the first message I wanted to speak to because we were all heading deeper into the global COVID pandemic, and there was much uncertainty and increasing strain. So I have revised that first Insight with some new thoughts.

In the background at that time was an issue I had at a company conference pre-COVID. There were a few hundred people, dense PowerPoint presentations, no breaks except lunch, and about a third of the attendees were on their phones. I knew what I needed, and that was to close my eyes: to breathe consciously, enabling a short mental break, after which I felt much relief and more focus. I also knew the drive home would be about two hours which ended up being four.

The next day I got a call from the person I reported to who happened to have "seen me" and who let me know it was unacceptable to have closed my eyes. Awkwardly, I felt like a scolded child. I've thought about that from time to time in the context of it being common to push ourselves without a break. It seems to me the unsustainability of a no-break mindset has consequences quite the opposite of the engagement and sustainable performance that we all desire.

The gift of that experience highlights how important it is to take a break and say when a break is needed. It's ok to close your eyes. It's ok to take a break or ask for help.

Rest, in micro or macro form, is a high-performance activity. Great athletes do rest exceptionally well. Our experience of sight requires up to 30% of our brain activity. Closing our eyes provides immediate rest for our brain.

And if we breathe out longer than an in-breath, we trigger our body's natural relaxation response: balanced breathing, an equal count on inhaling and exhaling, calms and restores balance.

Now more than ever, there is recognition of and appreciation for frontline health workers. Maybe we could all think of ourselves as frontline workers and offering essential services. As parents with kids at home or elderly parents, we can feel the need to be activated to help.

We are essential to many people in our network. And maybe not just at this time, but all the time is it vital to recognize the need to be ok with closing our eyes, taking a break if we feel exhausted from it all, or feel we are languishing.

Bessel van der Kolk is an expert on trauma, and years ago, he wrote a book called "The Body Keeps the Score." Recently he spoke about how this pandemic has elements of trauma and four ideas of how to cope.

1. Create structure. Having a schedule feels like a sense of control, known vs. the unknown world right now.
2. Renew connections. The harshest thing we can do to another human being is exile or solitary confinement; this pandemic has been a bit like that for some. Connection is embedded in our "DNA" as a must-have to be healthy. Do everything possible for connection and communication - make a goal of connecting each day with friends, healthily utilizing Facebook as an example.
3. Movement and engagement. Move your body. Trauma immobilizes us. Therefore, do things that mobilize us. Walks in nature we know are uplifting for us.
4. Celebrate competencies. If you love painting, paint if you love cooking, cook, and share recipes. Make online zoom dinners—re-experience joy in things you love to do.

I liken the benefits of closing our eyes to straightening out a wobble when driving tired or regaining focus when finding we are drifting through our day. Closing our eyes or taking a break is restorative and can be done anywhere, except, of course, in that car example! And it is a great transition tool to move skilfully and mindfully from one task to another. Benefits of Microbreaks

Here's the idea:

- Sitting with feet flat on the floor. Knees at ease positioned above our ankles.
- Allowing the chair to hold the weight of our upper body fully.
- Back straight but not rigid. Like sitting in a relaxed but dignified position.
- Chest out a bit. Shoulders relaxed and allowed to fall back.
- Neck relaxed. Head straight above our neck to minimize any strain.
- That position is most likely to, at the same time, bring a sense of calm and energy.
- Breathing in as deeply as comfortable and allowing a slow, long exhale, ideally through your nose. Even three breaths will feel better.

We have little information about how others are coping these days—let us be on the side of compassion and kindness to others and ourselves. Hang in there.

Insight Fifty-Four:
It's Ok for Me to Take A Break

Busy week. Big job simplifying my book notes today, amplified my energy to keep it going. More to do before I go for a long run. I'll be back next week with Insight 55!

Leaving you with a few quotes I like ….

Gratitude
"Piglet noticed that even though he had a very small heart, it could hold a rather large amount of gratitude." - A.A. Milne

Awareness
"Until you make the unconscious conscious, it will direct your life and you will call it fate." Carl Jung:

Dwell on Good Stuff
"Learn to keep the door shut, keep out of your mind, out of your office, and out of your world, every element that seeks admittance with no definitive helpful end in view." George Matthews Adam

Kindness
"Do all the good you can, by all the means you can, in all the ways you can, in all the places you can, at all the times you can, to all the people you can, as long as ever you can." - John Wesley, 1703–1791

Be well. It feels better.
226

Insight Fifty-Five:
Is It Fate?

I decided a few months ago to read my weekly Insight to my mom over the phone before I send it out. She always has something valuable to add.

I was driving home from the country and called her. She was quick to ask about last week's Insight, about which I hadn't called her. I told her I took a break and sent out a short letter with four quotes. The one example that came to mind to say to her was by Carl Jung, "Until you make the unconscious conscious, it will direct your life, and you will call it fate." So we ended up talking for an hour, mainly about fate.

We started with "is it all fate?" and "is everything predetermined"? Neither of us liked the idea of life driven by fate. Then I asked how it was that she met my dad and was that fate? I am alive and the father of three daughters only because my mom and dad were on the same bus almost 70 years ago. As my mom recalls, the bus could hold 45 people, and they're about 38 on it that Monday night, three being familiar; one was my dad. They chatted, decided to get off the bus, walk the rest of the way, "and by Friday, I had a date," she said.

I was asking a friend what he thought about fate. He didn't buy that it's all fate but did bring in the story of his parent's meeting. His dad was with a group of buddies hanging out on a street corner in a small city, and a convertible drove by with some young women in it. He pointed to the woman in the backseat and told his buddies that he would marry that girl. So what is that, if not fate?

Merriam Webster defines fate as the will or principle or determining cause by which things, in general, are believed to come to be as they are or events to happen as they do.

My mom told me that my dad said that it was "god-sent" when things went well.

Are these fateful meetings or situations sent or a setup? If so, by whom or by what means?

Then there is what some believe to be a law of attraction, based on the idea that thoughts are energetic and create or attract like energy: feeling good with positive thoughts attracts outcomes aligned to that. And feeling bad with thoughts of lack or want, make more of that. While there is no empirical evidence of that being a thing, I bet most people would say that is pretty much how it rolls.

I wondered out loud with my mom how she noticed my dad on a bus of 38 people. She said she was "interested" in him. Being interested implies being conscious. If she were unconscious of the fact he was there, you'd be doing something else right now.

228

Abraham Lincoln has been credited with the quote, "The best way to predict your future is to create it," and many others have said much the same and imply we can access free will.

My best shot at fate versus free will is that fate is a construct by us to explain meaningful or pivotal situations. Additionally, that fate or circumstance is a co-creating force with free will. It seems that the more conscious we are, the more free will we can access and apply, and the less fate is a factor.

But there still is the setup question, like my mom and dad being on the same bus or my friend's dad being on a particular street corner while the girl he would marry drove by. Who sets these up?

The question that is a little easier to navigate is what mindset are we in at any given moment and whether we can be aware of a setup?

My take is that at some level, my mom and dad happened to be similarly energetically "open" to finding a partner. Jonsey, while good at finding that magma displacement in Hunt for Red October, our internal "radar" operator is best in class.
Stuff happens all day long: a street is blocked, so go left or right, take this job or stay put, go out with this person or not. With a foundation in being aware or awake or conscious, our free will allows us to access the opportunity in random setups. Sometimes, there is an inexplicable knowing about a circumstance: purpose-built, pre-designed, and

229

ready to unfold fully in all its detail that we couldn't have begun to predict.

I also think that when we experience friction or disturbance, or turbulent thoughts, the "portal" closes in on us. For example, I had a plumber take out an iron pipe from the place we have in the country. It was old, corroded, and full of debris. The water was not flowing through the pipe cleanly— lots of resistance.

Is it fate? I think it's more like tuning in by being conscious of what we want, noticing with minimal resistance so we can capitalize on the stuff that happens all day long.

Be well. May you consciously direct your life so you can call it destiny.

Insight Fifty-Six:
The Overview Effect

I was listening to the BBC the other day, and there was a discussion about Frank White, who interviewed about 50 astronauts and, based on those insights, coined the term Overview Effect. White's book The Overview-Effect describes the profound effect and cognitive shift by looking at the Earth from above it.

One insight was that there are no boundaries between nations from space, one unique place we all share. The only distinctions from space are water and land.

There is no place like home, says Dorothy about Kansas. And although it is destined we explore space further to inhabit it, there is no place like our home in the known universe we all can share.

One astronaut recalls the first time looking out the window from space and seeing the Earth and saying his view was a 'heart-stopper" and compared the experience to looking over the edge of the Grand Canyon versus looking at pictures.

Another astronaut put his thumb up in his sightline to cover the Earth and was struck by the comparative vast emptiness and darkness everywhere else. Life on our planet is exclusive, and none other exists as far as we know. It's not hard to get a sense of the shift in thinking one would have by seeing Earth from space. The most precious thing we all share.

Another common thing we share on Earth is a circular exchange with nature. For example, every plant and tree releases oxygen. We collectively breathe in oxygen and give back our breathing waste of carbon dioxide, which trees need: neither would exist without the other.

A good friend I admire once said, "there are no minorities." But we have a terrible history of creating little and big suffering related to differences and separateness. So some might say yes, but it's very complex to unwind fully.

I think we are moving in the right direction even though we are still relatively young and still trying to figure it out:
- In our current form, we have been around for about 200,000 years.
- Our human ancestors showed up about 15 million years ago.
- Fish have been around for about 500 million years.
- Life began 4.2 billion years ago.

Last week in London, Ontario, a guy jumped a curb to run into a family of five Muslims, killing four. I don't even know where to begin in expressing how awful and disturbing that is to me.

This week, the interview about the Overview Effect that can shift a person's mindset and then hearing about the tragedy in London both got my attention. I wonder what it will take to move even more of us to an overview effect of sorts to see the precious nature of every life?

A few years ago, I went to a Compassionate Leadership Summit in Seattle. One of the sessions I signed up for was about emotional intelligence. Before starting the session, as everyone was getting settled, I noticed a gregarious guy beside me was pretty loud as he introduced himself all around. I found that a bit off-putting. As it happened, right off the bat, we were asked to pair up for an exercise. Everyone around me found a pair quickly except him and me. "Jeez, not this guy," I thought.

But as these things roll, in my experience, he was the perfect partner. The exercise was to share something hard we had in our life. One speaks, the other listens, and then switches. That guy had hard stuff to deal with, just like me. Ultimately, we became closer even as strangers before, simply listening to each other and realizing we had that hard stuff in common.

Common Humanity
A traditional approach to feeling a sense of shared humanity is to consider:

- "This person has feelings and emotions, just like me."
- "This person has been sad, hurt, or angry, just like me."
- "This person has experienced pain and suffering, just like me."
- "This person has experienced joy and happiness, just like me."
- "This person wishes to be healthy and loved, just like me."

We share one planet and a lot of life on it: many different species, but we represent just one. The cognitive shift can be that there is a oneness about us, more alike than different.

The overview effect can make us feel more similar than different because we all have problems, joys, hopes, and dreams. And this effect can be just enough to create a pause before a mindless reaction and feel through compassion that that person is imperfect, just like me, and wants to be happy, just like me.

What is absent sometimes, however, is the awareness of oneness. But through awareness, the apparent separateness and significant differences can then be seen as an illusion. Just like a rude awakening, that we were mistaken.
Keep in mind that we are more alike than different. Maybe not so complex.

Insight Fifty-Seven:
Automaticity – "Who Was Just driving?"

The other day I was on a long drive and called one of my brothers. We had a long, good talk. Although on a hands-free system, I was a bit freaked out to realize I don't remember much of the last hour of the drive. And who is driving our life?

When I learned to drive, it was different: key in the ignition, seat belt, check behind before I back up, watch for oncoming traffic, proceed cautiously, signal, turn off signal, keep monitoring rearview mirror and side mirrors on and on. The conscious part now is getting in the car, and the rest is mainly habitual and automatic.

We all learned to walk. And when we see a toddler learning, it's clumsy. One chubby leg has to be shifted forward from the hip and planted on the ground, heel first, rolling through to the toe. The process of walking is called a double pendulum strategy. And as if briefly balancing on that forward leg and not tipping over, lifting the other leg and bringing it past the other. Lots of falls trying to master that tricky maneuver. We all got the hang of it.

Automaticity is the capacity to do things with a low level of thinking: a habit or pattern learned and, through repetition, becomes automatic or unconscious. So great for the most part that we don't have to relearn walking, speaking, or playing the violin every time.

"We first make our habits, and then our habits make us." - John Dryden.

Much of the time, our thought patterns are automatic, like judgments and biases: sometimes, we do stuff or say stuff out of habit.

Research has shown it takes about a tenth of a second to judge someone's honesty must be an evolutionary survival strategy. If we don't have to think when reacting unconsciously, we can use our conscious mind for other things.

And like the centipede, who, when asked by the toad how it walks, is immobilized by consciously reflecting on it, lots of time we become at risk if we think about what is automatic. Being in a flow state or high performance is more about allowing than it is about thinking. If we did disrupt the flow, it would spoil the performance.

On the other hand, some automatic behaviour doesn't help. Unconscious emotional reactivity may seem like a fast and effective tool but often is destructive. Negative thought patterns don't help. Reacting unskillfully for some may be a pattern with consequences of which they are largely unaware.

A study I have referred to before about the significant gap between leaders ranking themselves very highly and employees preferring a pay cut to have that Leader stay on is, in my view, part of the risk of unconscious behaviour.

A fundamental way to shift to "above the line" conscious communication and behaviour are to practice noticing or bringing our attention to something. The natural capacity we all have for paying attention that is trainable is mindfulness.

We could ask ourselves how it is going for us, acknowledge the good, and be open to learning in areas where our thoughts and behaviours aren't getting us what we want.

An Advisor in a Branch I was the Leader of was perplexed when Assistant after Assistant would not be happy and eventually left. The turnover was disruptive to his business. He was uncommunicative, showed little appreciation for what his team did, rarely came out of his office, and was intimidating. He had no idea.

It takes some courage, but with the **intention** of better outcomes for all, **discernment** of thoughts, and a **deliberate** approach, we can lift the unconscious to our conscious mind. If we shift from the binds of automaticity in areas that don't serve us, we can experience more freedom and flexibility.

Enriching our lives can come from tuning into the world around us, like taking a different route home, listening more, brushing our teeth with the other hand.

There might be more to see, a better view, by challenging some of our automatic patterns in an enlightened perspective.

Take the high road. The view is better.

Insight Fifty-Eight:
Accountability. Will It Help?

I enjoy physical fitness. It makes me feel good. During the COVID pandemic, I wanted to exercise regularly. Some days I didn't do anything,

There were a lot of days when the internal dialogue was, "today I will work out. I can get this done." But often, there was disappointment at the end of the day.

I have felt my motivation and drive wane during the last year, which doesn't feel good. So as an antidote, I try to acknowledge the good facts of what I have done. Self-compassion is helpful when we are not where we want to be.

I reconnected online with Paul, a friend I've known for years. Because of our swimming background, a natural question to ask each other was, "are you working out?" Unfortunately, we both had the same disappointing answer, "not as much as we want."

Paul seemed to want to get back on his Peloton. I wanted to get going on more chin-ups, so we formed an easy partnership. The outcome for both of us has been considerably more than we were doing.
The American Society of Training and Development found "that people are 65 percent

likely to meet a goal after committing to another person", and that is a big leg up on getting the rest of the way!

The challenge of going on our own revealed in a Harvard study is that we are naturally distracted about 47% of the time. In an article referencing the research, authors Killingsworth and Gilbert write, "A human mind is a wandering mind, and a wandering mind is an unhappy mind. And the ability to think about what is not happening is a cognitive achievement that comes at an emotional cost. Wandering mind not a happy mind – Harvard Gazette

The fact that we can think about what is not happening is both good and bad. The good thing is that we can review things in the past, learn, anticipate the future, and skillfully plan.

But we aren't always in that optimal state. When we ruminate about the past and worry about the future, we create stress that is a distraction and resistance to allowing more great in our lives. At a high level, there is an epidemic of stress and anxiety. At an individual level, when mentally traveling to the past or into the future, we weaken our ability to get the right stuff done.

When we purposely grow the time we spend in the present moment, with an orientation to action through accountability, the past or the future seem less relevant. And sometimes that mental time travel deludes us into imagining the big goal has to be all figured out, or all those future chin-ups are too much to bear right now when all we have to do is just one thing now.

One thing now, and we are winning.

Recently, I reconnected with a friend who has been coaching and consulting for years. We decided to help each other with business goals. Our call ended with an agreement to share our big picture destination and our one-month objectives. I'm not sure each of us would have jumped to that clarity as quickly in our heads and on our own.

The connection and common direction lifted each of us to a higher place of inspired action: she added "fierce" to accountability, taking the process up a notch.

With accountability, we can get better access to now, the only place we can act and, therefore, allow what we genuinely want to get done. That feels good: our lives experience expansion in accountability.

We don't always need a buddy. There are plenty of things we just get done: a private dream can be powerful enough for us to be fully accountable, like being accountable to a loved one or an important project at work.

But in those times where it matters, it's ok to ask for help. We don't have to be alone in the challenge. Accountability is part of habit formation. And it doesn't have to be complicated or time-consuming.

Telling someone else is a different commitment than just telling yourself because nobody will hear you except your conscience.

A basic formula could be:
- Find someone who, as a partner, makes you feel our future is nearer than before.
- Decide what we want?
- Determine when it will be done or for how long we will do it?
- Decide how the communication will happen" A regular meeting, a text, or a call?

Motivation is the fuel or energy that supports the actions we want to take. The very best kind of motivation is intrinsic: those things that give us fulfillment and satisfaction. And being in the energy of intrinsic motivation is very good for our wellbeing.

See the work.
Create accountability for the work.
Avoid the misery.

If we do one thing right now, we are closer than before, which is excellent.

Insight Fifty-Nine:
More Eustress the Better

When I was a teenager, I swam competitively. I worked hard and often competed: it's easy for me to imagine an example of a swim meet from the collective experience of all of them.

I would try to arrive early. If I didn't get to the pool early, I would notice a feeling of stress building. If that happened, I would attempt to rein it in. Once at the pool and on deck, I would take in the environment and energy, say hi to a few people but mainly begin activating a sense of intention and energy control.

I would check the heat sheets to see when my first race was and what heat I was in. I would often feel some stress in my gut, so I would lock in the heat and lane numbers in my head, rein in the pressure and get in quickly for the warm-up.

Usually, I wasn't in the first event, so I would sit in the stands with the team and wait after the warm-up. Then, as the event got closer, I would find my stress rising again but rein it in by going for a walk and keeping loose. Then, I might go to the washroom or maybe get a short drink or a bit of food.

Staying loose and ready was the game. I would often find a quiet place to let my body connect with my mind and make final preparations for the "business" I was about to take care of.

As it got to be 5 or 10 minutes away from the start, I would shake myself awake and take some long inhales and short fast exhales to get activated. Then, "swimmers, take your blocks ... " and the gun starts the race.

From the moment I woke up on the swim meet day, my work was to monitor the inevitable stress and the embedded energy to check it, hold it, prepare it, and then unleash it.

Hans Selye, a Hungarian doctor, became an expert in stress, starting with a book published in 1956 called *The Stress of Life, and twenty* years later, Selye coined the term eustress. "Eu" is a Greek prefix for good, and eustress became a term to differentiate from the standard and most emphasized connotation of stress that it is all bad.

Indeed, chronic bad stress triggers a long list of very nasty health issues, but not all stress is bad. For example, getting out of bed and immediately being subject to the power of gravity causes stress to our bodies. But the stressor of any movement up to high-performance exercise plus rest is the only way our muscles grow.

Eustress (good stress) characteristics (*Mills, Reiss, and Dombeck 2018*):
- It lasts in the short term.
- Energizes and motivates.
- Perceived as something within our coping ability.
- It feels exciting.
- It increases focus and performance.

Distress (bad stress) characteristics:
- Lasting in the short as well as in the long term.
- Triggering anxiety and concern.
- Surpassing our coping abilities.
- Generating unpleasant feelings.
- Decreasing focus and performance.
- Contributing to mental and physical problems.

If a few of us were sitting around a fire on a Saturday night about 100,000 years ago and someone noticed a big bush moving nearby, all those who freaked out and ran away at full speed survived the possibility a massive predator was looking for a late-night snack. Anyone who thought maybe it was just the wind was the snack.

Some distress from stress is appropriate and has been a good friend to us. Our bodies have evolved to have the stress response triggered for 90 seconds, after which the adrenaline and otherwise toxic cortisol are flushed out of our system so we can calmly go back to the fire pit minus our friend.

It is helpful for us to know that should we feel a high level of stress, our system still has that built-in 90-second window in which we can watch it happen, feel it happen and then have it fade away. Then, if we still feel high stress after that, we can listen to our thoughts to see how they drive us to stay in the stress lane. With practice, we can manage stress for our good instead of it driving the show.

A long-term study in the US of 30,000 people revealed that those who viewed stress as bad experienced a higher mortality rate than others who viewed stress as good. The learning in the study was that how we perceive stress is a matter of life or death. Those who perceive stress as a positive can expect a boost in the immune system functioning, improved performance, and optimized learning.

We can better recognize the physiology of our bodies when experiencing stress like our heart racing, tension, and an upset stomach and reframe those sensations as real-time, precise, and helpful information.

Stress is energy, and we could ask ourselves in this shift of perspective what we can do to turn this stress into eustress. And the highest form of eustress, the most optimized state of human performance, is the state of flow, the place where stress and capacity to execute intersect.

The next time we feel a high degree of stress, we can pause and listen to the rich bio-feedback and see if we can use the information for our good.

Insight Sixty:
One Mind and It's Mine

My Dad was a financial analyst in the investment business. The most significant part of his career was with a national supermarket chain: he knew the food business well. His underlying training was as a Chartered Accountant: he also knew the business of numbers well.

As a financial analyst, he successfully brought together his experience in the food business and his training in numbers to cover the large food companies in Canada. He wrote a weekly research piece he called Financial Alerts. This piece went out broadly to the investment community and his firm's institutional clients.

My Dad entitled one weekly Alert, "The One Asshole Theory." He discovered that a competing supermarket planned to build a large store close to a competitor in a mature residential market. His position was that the success of that new store or return on investment would be limited, and likely that the current store would suffer as well.

His rationale was that by adding a new store to the market, people aren't going to all of a sudden eat more because we each only have one asshole. His weekly Alerts weren't always so colourful but often were quite to the point.

248

Another thing we all have in common is having one mind. And just because a business wants us to consume news, podcasts, books, clothes, courses and get at us by online advertising that pops up right in the middle of an article we are reading to enchant powerfully doesn't mean we have to.

Consuming more is the call to all our senses. As a result, our time and attention, our mind, is the target of an enormous number of big and small companies.

We only have one mind, and it's ours.

A few years ago, I was driving with a radio on. The news hour came up, but I didn't feel like listening to all the bad news worldwide, so I switched channels. That was fine until the news came on that channel, and I heard similar headlines. It dawned on me then that the media has and will feed us whatever they choose. For the most part, I used to listen to the news like unconsciously eating, just throwing down the hatch whatever was put in front of me. I have come to be much more selective about my diet of news.

The stuff we get pushed on us is endless. While the brain is a stunning piece of equipment, it requires care and maintenance to function optimally now and for the long term. If we get overwhelmed, plugged up, feel paralyzed by too much choice (Paradox of Choice) or feel a sense of brain freeze, we can also experience anxiety and stress.

Because there is nothing more important than feeling good, it's helpful to look for an antidote to mental indigestion we can sometimes experience if stuff is stuck and there is no flow. If we pay attention, stress can be good information to find a way to bring more control and choice for our minds; otherwise, we might go out of our minds.

Some ways to wrestle control over our attention:

Silence is a big trend in global wellness to counter all the noise, and digital "noise" to support better focus and memory.

Being in nature reduces eye strain from prolonged computer use.

Exercise creates a direct link to improved cognitive ability, particularly attention.

Mindfulness meditation neurologically trains self-regulation.

Structure & Intention – knowing what you are doing and why will reduce the pull of distracting forces.

Rest – Healthy rest restores and supports our ability to make good choices.

250

We must work to win in this game of attention to the right thing.

We only have one mind, and it's ours. Care for it wisely. And be careful what you pack in there.

Insight Sixty-One
Enjoy this Day

At some point, as the week progresses, I ask myself, "what do I want to say this week?" Sometimes I pick up on something I've read or someone has said that triggers a message that I want to pass along, which happened twice this week. I wrote a letter that was ready to go but will send that next week because something else quickly got my attention this morning.

I woke up feeling out of sorts, a little down and slow at getting at my morning writing routine. Not getting at my practice amplified some thoughts that maybe I wasn't writing as much I could be. That felt bad like an emerging dark cloud: a morning downward spiral instead of the upward spiral I intend to create each day.

So, I decided to take the girls (my two red labs) to a nearby park for the regular 7:30 gathering of owners and dogs. I saw Jeff, who has become a friend through some nicely human and authentic conversations. I told him I was feeling down this morning and realized that I had quite a significant day moving two projects ahead yesterday.

He is an accomplished musician, and my story resonated with him in that sometimes he "sacrifices" some highlights or successes by being

252

drawn to what he hasn't done. We reflected on the mind's propensity to take us places like one day an emerging cloud takes over the light, and another day the light burns away the darkness: the "weather" of our mind can create good days and bad days.

We decided we would have a beer soon and undoubtedly explore this topic to flatten or reduce the amplitude of the waves of emotions: more precisely, to keep the highs and minimize the time in the lows.

Another friend arrived with her dog. After the talk with Jeff, I was already way back up the curve from earlier, and I asked my friend what is most outstanding in her life these days. She thought that was a good question to reflect on.

However, finding the good was tricky this morning for her as she revealed that a friend was in a medically induced coma with internal bleeding and possibly brain damage. And further that her friend's 13-year-old daughter died in the same boating accident just two days ago. It is uncertain if the mother will recover or what state she will be in if she does.

It was an accident where a boat "T-boned" another on a large lake involving six people. From one boat, one mother is dead, and three kids survive. From the other boat, the other mother is in a coma, and her daughter is gone.

I listened to my friend as she explored her thoughts about wanting to help and not being able to and how the daughter, a vibrant young girl, had a promising tennis future and did some fantastic charity work.

Great futures ended in an instant.

"The most terrifying fact about the universe is not that it is hostile but that it is indifferent; but if we can come to terms with this indifference and accept the challenges of life within the boundaries of death ... our existence as a species can have genuine meaning and fulfillment. However vast the darkness, we must supply our own light." - Stanley Kubrick

We walked back from the park together, reflecting on how one can hold a tragedy's pain and hold good things too. And how tragic events can serve as reminders to enjoy each day because of our own mortality.

Some people might say, 'Today was a great day because someone bought what I was selling.' Or "today was a lousy day because it rained."

Death is so final, like a light switch. It's shocking to the system even if expected.
A friend of a friend died recently waiting for a liver transplant. My friend coincidently has been raising money and awareness for organ donations. Of

254

course, she was sad about the passing of her friend, and she also allowed herself to feel good with a renewed purpose for the foundation work she is doing.

We can grieve. We can care for those still here. We can be sad. And we can honour a life lost by fueling purpose and meaning in our lives and enriching others' lives through that energy.

Enjoy this day, no matter the "weather."

Insight Sixty-Two:
Validation is a Superpower

I am taking a 12-week course called Family Connections offered by the Sashbear Foundation to parents and other caregivers helping loved ones cope with mental health issues. Three of the twelve weeks are on the topic of validation.

One of our deepest needs as humans is to feel understood. So, validation is like a superpower, but what is it?

Validation is the language and behaviour of understanding and acknowledging another person's emotional experience, making them feel heard and understood. The opposite would be invalidation which sometimes happens unconsciously by non-listening, rejection of the other's feelings, or judgment of emotions.

Validation doesn't mean we must agree or condone another's feelings, just that we are genuine in our understanding of how they feel. We seek external validation to feel understood and connected, and self-validation is a healthy practice of recognizing and acknowledging our thoughts and feelings as valid.
Validation: "That must feel so bad." Or "I think I can understand how you would feel." Or a simple

behavioural validation like a hand on a shoulder or a hug goes a long way.

Invalidation: "Oh, it's not a big deal, just work harder." Or "I told you it wouldn't work." Or "Hey, get over it."

Notice which one feels better.

Each week of the program, there is homework. For example, last week, the assignment was (1) Make a validating statement once a day to a person, (2) What behaviour do you tend to validate the most and least. And (3) Count how many times in one day someone validates you.

There was some excellent discussion on the first two questions, and when it came to answering the 3rd question, there was silence until one person said zero and another said once a day. The point made by the third question was to suggest that our world is mainly un-validating.

Validation outcomes:
- The core element in productive dialogue.
- Builds trust and rapport.
- Enhances the self-respect of the recipient.
- Decreases anger.
- It makes other parties feel optimistic about the relationship.

I was struck in that session by the gap between these excellent potential outcomes and the degree to which people validate others.

"When someone really hears you without passing judgment on you, without trying to take responsibility for you, without trying to mold you, it feels damn good!" - Carl Rodgers.

You might have heard of Dr. John Gottman, an American psychologist who has studied thousands of couples and claims to be able to predict with 94% certainty which ones will end in divorce.

One early study was with 130 newly married couples observed during a day on a weekend retreat. He noticed partners making seemingly random comments like, "Wow, look at that car" or "I enjoyed the meal."

Gottman called these verbal connections "bids," and if the partner responded engagingly with something like, "yes, that is a nice car," or "I'm so glad you enjoyed your meal," he called these responses "turning towards." On the other hand, if there was no response or the response negative, he termed those "turning away from the bid."

Gottman found that those who were divorced had "turned towards the bids" only 33% of the time in a six-year follow-up study: only three of ten bids were met with interest and engagement from the partner. However, after six years, those still married had almost nine out of ten "turn towards the bids," thereby richly meeting each other's emotional needs.

258

I encourage you to watch this funny video (< 2 minutes), which perfectly "nails" what validation is and isn't! It's Not About the Nail - Bing video.

We are humans at home outside work and humans at work too. So how can validation make things better on the job? For starters, not validating is expensive. Although recognition is only one aspect of validation, a Gallup poll in the US reveals that only one in three employees is praised or recognized. Those other two-thirds were twice as likely to quit within the following year. Conversely, we can assume there is a strong correlation between validation and engagement.

At work, validation can apply to coaching performance, building rich communication with clients and partners, dealing effectively with emotional people, and uplifting relationships one by one to support a tremendous overall culture.

Imagine a team becoming intentional about validation by considering Gottman's data of almost nine of ten bids being positive in a lasting relationship and how that could fuel sustainable high performance in a team at work.
Validation elements:
- Being present. Paying attention and actively listening to the other person.
- Reflecting or acknowledging the emotional experience non-judgmentally.
- Show tolerance for the other person.

- Act with radical genuineness.
- Be vulnerable, which is a form of validation. Like, "me too."

Validation genuinely offered will nail down a better relationship!

Insight Sixty-Three:
Looks, Liver & Heart

You could install an Endless Pool in your basement or backyard. These rectangular pools have powerful jets at one end to keep the swimmer in place: like swimming against the current. But, of course, we all have experienced swimming against the current from time to time.

Unexpected currents of life might be a health issue we didn't ask for and certainly don't want. Let's say you find out you need part of a liver, or you will die. And let's say you find yourself on the short lucky list and get part of a liver, and you get back your life. So now what?

"Tell me, what is it you plan to do with your one wild and precious life?" Mary Oliver

I've seen this quote before, but frankly, it never quite took on its whole meaning until a few months when I met a young lady named Jillian and decided to help her.

Five years ago, Jillian needed part of a liver and luckily got one. She does everything she can to welcome someone else's organ into her body with self-care, diet, and a unique outlook on how precious her life is.

As I understand it, her friend Grey, another lucky list survivor, and Jillian were kicking around big dreams, and he suggested they swim across Lake Ontario together. Lake Ontario is one of five Great Lakes that the US and Canada share.

The traditional swim route across Lake Ontario (51km) was set by Marilyn Bell (now DiLascio), a pioneer of open water swimming who completed the previously considered impossible swim in 1954.

When you get a new lease on life, there's s an opportunity to go large. We should all aspire to go large by realizing we've been on the lucky list from day one.

Grey has had a few challenges with his transplant, so Jillian was left to fulfill the dream. The good thing for Jillian is that Grey has a huge heart in addition to a new liver and shares his "all-in on living" attitude to support Jillian.

So, this big, bold idea takes shape, and there we are, waiting on the south shore of Lake Ontario at the mouth of the Niagara River to take Jillian north to Toronto and, specifically, to Marilyn Bell Park.

I have helped with 20 or more open water swims, primarily across Lake Ontario. I made three attempts, two of which were successful. However, it was hard for me to think of a better team assembled to support Jillian.

The Stage:
- An excellent, committed navigator captained one large, lead powerboat.
- Two large rubber inflatable boats called Zodiacs.
- Crew: Swimmer, Coach, Pacers (They get in and rotate swims to support the swimmer), two medical professionals, Zodiac drivers, a dietician, and a Swim Master (me) to ensure rules and safety protocols are adhered to.

The Looks:
Jillian. At the start, standing in the water looking across a Great Lake with no idea what challenges await. But, prepared simply with a bathing suit, cap, and goggles, Jillian looks like she is stronger than whatever she might encounter. She is also taking in the knowledge of excellent preparedness and the rich support from family and friends. It is 11:01 pm, and she leans into the dark water and begins the dream.

Lynne is the dietician and looks after feeding Jillian. The look from Lynne is of an unwavering commitment to Jillian's fuel needs during the swim, for however long it takes. In addition, Lynne emits care and compassion.

Zach is Jillian's husband. He has a look of deep connection with Jillian and exudes competence. Zach is not worried or afraid for Jillian: wholly and completely believing in her capacity to do this. He is her foremost cheerleader from his heart and vocally on the swim.

Crissy is a Zodiac driver and Paramedic. Her look was of focus and professional knowledge of the risks. And from a personal high-performance sports background, Crissy knew what this was all about: she brought clarity of intent.

Grey is a pacer. One of the best looks I saw was Grey completing a pacing stint and getting back in the boat with an expression of joy, like coming down at Christmas and finding two trees. It looked like he hadn't just experienced being in the water with Jillian but was the experience. Like the expansive water and horizon, the care and friendship for Jillian, his commitment to being there, all one beautiful experience. Grey brought aliveness.

Steve was a Pacer and Zodiac driver. Despite a busy business and family life, Steve's look was one of being there fully for Jillian. Like knowing precisely, the privilege to witness this event and honouring that to bring all, he has to help with excellence in both duties. Steve brought amazement at what was possible.

Mayur - Medical Advisor. Another top best look of the swim was of Mayur responding to information about an alternate, shorter, untraditional, and in all ways a less than destination given quite significant challenges with currents near the end. However,

Mayur's look was at the same time medically and safety based and emotionally pure. He was too polite and professional to say what I felt in his look, which was, "no fucking way are we going to any other destination than Marilyn Bell Park, the one Jillian deserves to go to and can make it to."

Kat was a Zodiac driver. Kat's look was of the heart. Her interest in people and coming with heart was so evident in all the ways she contributed. Whether it was bringing a powerful positivity, cleaning up, driving supplies or people, or a simple conversation in the hours throughout the swim, it was all done with heart.

Vanessa was a last-minute addition as a pacer. Her look was of childlike joy to be there in the water with Jillian. She brought enthusiasm, commitment, and skill to her pacing Jillian.

Kyle was a social media contributor, photographer, and drone Captain. His look was of astonishment at the magnitude of the challenge and commitment of the crew to help Jillian fulfill her dream.

Benoit is Jillian's Coach and has a long and successful background of swimming and coaching experience. He has helped Jillian with her training. Benoit brought all that background plus a comradeship and connection for being on the lucky list too. Benoit had a look of quiet, knowing, and intelligence of Jillian's capacity to do this by monitoring her pace and progress to complete the swim.

Jillian's last look. After hours of swimming against the current off the Toronto shoreline in the final 15 km, in profound fatigue like she has never experienced before, she lifts her head 500 metres to go and hears the gathered crowd roaring with encouragement. I see a wave of emotion roll over her. She treads water for a moment taking in the sound and what she is about to accomplish, clearly overcome with all of it.

She then tenderly puts her down, lifts one aching arm after the other out of the water on her final strokes to the finish.

At the finish, I am in a Zodiac right beside Jillian and, in her last stroke at 5:37 pm, after 18 hours and 36 minutes, I see her reach out and touch the wall at Marilyn Bell Park.

Her final look was as if three little words meant the world to her, "I did it."

Insight Sixty-Four:
Pilot or Passenger?

Breathing is vital. Plain and simple. No breath, and after about 30 seconds for most of us, our body starts to freak out.

I must say, for a long time, I've taken breathing for granted. I don't have to do anything, and my body keeps breathing. Nice. I exert myself, and I breathe heavily to compensate, and when relaxed, I breathe easily. Excellent.

I could sit back as a passenger and see how the ride goes enduring the turbulence from time to time or, maybe I'll head up front to fly this baby.

All organs operate automatically, so it is easy to let breathing be unconscious and passive. But breath can be like a throttle. We can use our breath to communicate with the vagus nerve, which empowers and depowers our organs. The vagus what?

The vagus nerve is the longest nerve we have, and it runs from the brain stem to our abdomen and, along the way, regulates most of the significant organs in our body.

For example, about 90% of our brain's output power is for the vagus nerve to regulate heart rate, digestion, kidney and liver functioning, and other vital organs. And the vagus nerve is part of the autonomic nervous system. And the two critical parts of the autonomic nervous system are the sympathetic and parasympathetic systems.

Sympathetic nervous system (SNS) - Prepares us for stress by increasing the heart rate, increasing blood flow to the muscles, and decreasing blood flow to the skin: stress response.
Parasympathetic nervous system (PNS) – Calms our body right down and undoes the work of the fight or flight mode with rest, being restored and allowing healthy digestion to resume: relaxation response.

On a micro-level, an in-breath triggers the SNS, and the out-breath triggers the PNS. Thus, breathing is effectively like being a pilot and having a firm grip on the control stick connected to the vagus nerve that sends the respective message down the line. Faster, longer in-breaths activate the system, and slower, longer exhales calm the system.

It seems that as the time from my first inhale gets longer and the time to my last exhale gets shorter, breathing well has been more and more of interest to me.
Several years ago, I ended up switching beds with my youngest daughter, who headed to the big bed in the middle of the night. My middle daughter had a sleepover guest, and they were in a bunk bed.

When I woke up in the other bed in the same room, my daughter and her friend were sitting on the side of the lower bunk staring at me. The guest said, "you sleep weird." And my daughter said, "Daddy, you stopped breathing a few times last night." I might have laughed that off and carried on, but I decided to go to a sleep clinic and found I had a mild case of sleep apnea which I dealt with, and now I enjoy better sleep.

"Ya, I snore so loud apparently the house shakes. But, hey, it doesn't bother me!" Good sleep is critical to wellbeing and has long-term not-so-funny consequences if ignored. The author mentioned below refers to the "horrendous" health effects of snoring and sleep apnea.

Another breathing well nudge was after seeing a naturopath about an issue. He asked me how my breathing was going. While I was thinking about how to answer that question, he said, "there is quite a lot of research on breathing lately." So I took note and have become much more conscious of how I breathe.

Recently I read and am now reviewing a deeply researched book by James Nestor called Breath - New Science of a Lost Art. Nestor's book is a bestseller on several lists and translated into 30 languages. So it seems as though a lot of people are interested in breathing.

What's the fuss, and can there be that much said about breathing? As it turns out, Nestor has about 250 pages of words to say about breathing.

Some key points Nestor makes:
Shut your mouth: Breathe as much from your nose as possible. It turns out there are much better outcomes from nose breathing for our health.

Fully exhale: The lungs or "engine" works better when we practice fully exhaling.

Chew: Eat stuff that requires chewing, which helps sustain sinus cavities, strong jaws, and straight teeth.

How we breathe: Studies show that 5.5 seconds per breath or 11 seconds round trip is optimal. To balance your system, try this for 2 or 3 minutes, and you'll find you have caused your body to move to a more calm, focused, and balanced place.

I was on a long zoom call this afternoon. One of the participants talked about how when he arrives from the city to his country place in a valley with very little development, he says, "here I can really breathe!"

Breathe well, Captain; it will make for a better trip!

Insight Sixty-Five:
Contemplation

Before my wife's birthday, I asked her what she wanted, and her response was unusual but memorable. She asked me to drive her around and wait while she did a bunch of little errands like returning an item or picking up something on hold.

She hopped out at each stop while I parked the car or circled the block. She had a good list, and we covered a lot of ground. She felt amazing to complete so many little things that until then were incomplete.

My observations are that getting stuff done feels great, and incompletions hold energy like it's waiting in reserve to be used to get it done. So the intended action gets stored up, consuming energy like a low load device taking a portion of the charge, causing a drain from the primary source.

The stuff to complete could be minor or significant activities or relationships or something we want to say.

When I was a Branch Manager, I had to deal with a particularly challenging guy and talk to him about his performance. Each time I went to speak to him, I had a plan of what I would say. And most times, I left frustrated that I hadn't fully gotten my message across.

Afterward, it was like an emotional echo in my mind was replaying the meeting and coming up with just the right thing to say or being self-critical of why I allowed the message to be incomplete.

So much energy is consumed by holding onto stuff in our minds that are undone or unsaid.

I read Fierce Conversations by Susan Scott (no relation), which helped me have more clean and clear conversations. As a result, I got better at the talks with this salesman. Two good things happened: (1) Little to no echo or ruminating after future meetings, and (2) the relationship significantly improved.

Completed conversations significantly reduce energy consumption.
A hundred years ago, a Lithuanian psychologist named Bluma Zeigarnik noticed that waiters recalled food orders not completed more clearly versus ones that had. Then she did a study with school kids where she gave them tasks in a limited amount of time like puzzles and math problems. Half the group was allowed to complete the tasks, and the other half was interrupted, resulting in incompletions.

Then, after an hour, the kids were asked to recall the tasks. About 12% of the kids could remember the completed tasks in the first group, while 80% of the second group remembered the uncompleted tasks.

The Zeigarnik Effect says that we tend to recall those things that are incomplete more than things completed. She further discovered that the timing of an interruption and the degree of connection to pride and self-esteem mattered to eventual completion.

People who are distracted at the beginning of a task have more of a challenge to persevere to completion. Those who invested action and thoughts longer in the task had higher rates of finishing when distracted. Also, if pride and self-esteem were at stake, people had higher completion rates after a distraction or interruption.

My conclusions are
- Our innate negativity bias plays into incompletions by the mind more naturally focused on things not done.
- Things left incomplete consume energy or have a cognitive load that can only be released by completing or discarding the task.
- It feels great to get stuff done.
- Feeling great is loaded with fuel for momentum and life expansion and has positive mental health attributes.
- Incompletions feel bad and bad is not good.

The Zeigarnik Effect is practical because it reminds us of something that needs to be done. To increase completions, we can get started and keep going as an antidote to potential interruptions. And the Zeigarnik Effect is evolutionarily based, as the most vital drive is survival; stuff undone still represents a risk in our minds, and stuff done doesn't matter anymore.

But from a desire to feel good more often, we can manage the tendency for the brain to stick to the bad, risky or incomplete by dwelling on the good.

"See the job, do the job, stay out of the misery." - Maharishi Mahesh Yogi.

It's a worthy aspiration to complete what is important and moves us forward to avoid disappointment. And at the root of these aspirations is a voice that is always calling us to a higher level and we should celebrate these completions, not forget them.

To respectfully uplift that quote, we could say, "See the job, do the job, savor each success."

Insight Sixty-six:
The Voice We Should Listen To

Yesterday I was thinking about what I want to say this week. First, two themes dropped in, then a third idea. But the fourth one was the best.

The fourth theme was an inner voice or message, maybe a gift. A gift would be an excellent way to describe it.

While ideas for what I want to say are bubbling up, I feel a little blocked, like tension or restriction, to execute one of the ideas because I have two unfinished things on my plate. So the limitation and conflict I felt was the interest in writing a full Insight today versus completing two projects.

Sometimes I get myself in these too much to do in not enough time predicaments. Sometimes I set myself up for not feeling good by trying to do too much: while I get some stuff done, it wasn't all of it, so I have little chance of feeling satisfied.

So, the inner voice gift was to write a short Insight and get the two projects done. And the clarity that I would feel much better if I got the two projects done than if I wrote a complete Insight and didn't finish the unfinished.

I'm getting better at listening. And once I decided what my priorities were for the day, I immediately felt uplifted and eager to get at them.

And noticing my internal energy went from low and stuck or overwhelmed (energy consumption) to feeling relief and eagerness at completing these two projects (energy creation)—transformed energy: nice.

We often get messages from inside about what to say or do now or what we need to do to feel better. So I think there is a lot of wisdom that bubbles up. And I want to keep working on listening well.

"There is a voice that doesn't use words." - Rumi.

Enjoy this day because there will never be another one just like it.

Insight Sixty-Seven:
It's Magic!

When I was a teenager, I swam competitively and increasingly saw the results from intention and effort. Then, at one point, I became aware of an upcoming Canadian Team trip to New Zealand for an international competition. So, I checked out the qualifying times for the events that I could swim pretty well and found that the 200-metre freestyle time was the most likely possibility.

Around that time, my dad gave me a book called The Magic of Believing by Claude Bristol, who wrote it in 1948. Of many different strategies to bring about what we want, the one that I used to help with my new goal of going to New Zealand was writing the dream down in precise terms on an index card.

I decided to qualify for the 200 freestyle, so I took the time I had to make and broke it down into four small goals of 50 metres each. Then I wrote five separate times, each of the 4 50 metre splits and the total time on the card.

I kept that index card with me in my wallet and looked at it frequently. My mind's reaction to it was interesting. For a while, when I would look at the card, thoughts arose of its impossibility which made sense, given I had never swum a 200-metre race that fast.

I kept looking at the goal splits each day. I also kept training hard. Finally, one day it dawned on me (a new series of thoughts-neuroplasticity in action) that I had swum as fast or faster in a single 50 metre race than any of the 50 splits that were on the card.

It was occurring to me that my goal was now plausible. It was fascinating to observe my thoughts move from impossible to plausible. And it was encouraging and fueled my intent and effort.

Then I began to reflect that the challenge isn't in swimming a lot faster; it would be in the endurance to put four 50 metre swims back-to-back. That different perspective made me more conscious and intentional of the training to be about endurance.

Now my goal was feeling possible.

A swim meet was approaching that would serve as an opportunity to qualify for the Canadian Team, so I entered the 200-metre freestyle.
Waiting behind my lane and as the previous heat finished, I heard the starter say, "Swimmers, take your blocks." I hopped up and shuffled to the front, wrapped my toes around the edge of the downward sloping starting block, and bent over in the ready position. The starter then fired the starting pistol, and off I went.

The dive was perfect, getting a good distance off the blocks, my entry was smooth and efficient, and my stroke was powerful and fast. Every 50 metres felt good. I was in a zone of non-thinking alignment between mind and body. There was no struggle, just swimming. I didn't experience fatigue. At the 175-meter mark, the last flip turn, I came off the wall strongly and finished with everything I had.

I didn't look up to the scoreboard when I touched the timing pads to finish the race because I knew I had made the time. I went back to my Team's area, and my coach congratulated me on a good swim. He confirmed I swam a personal best and made the qualifying time to go to New Zealand. When I looked later at the splits, they were precisely what I had written on the card except for the last 50 metres, which was two-tenths of a second faster.

Making Magic:
- An inspired dream or goal.
- Write clear, condensed, and precise points.
- Mental objection to that goal. Thought barriers that "say" it is impossible.
- Dwelling on the inspired goal overrides the negative narrative.
- Evidence arises to support the goal making it plausible.
- More evidence emerges, making the goal possible.
- The inspired dream becomes a reality.

In my experience, the reality of the completion of a goal isn't simply success and onto something else. Instead, the completion, little or big, activates an expansion mechanism that unfolds that makes the outcome magnitudes better and has effects beyond what one could imagine while previously and preciously holding that seed of a dream.

I think Bristol called his book The Magic of Believing because we can believe the stuff we want into our reality, and that's like magic!

Some might think the magic is out there but limited with only so much to go around. However, we are not separate from the magic, and it's not limited.

May you dream in that which you want by believing it is all possible.

Insight Sixty-Eight:
Field of Dreams

_____

This past week I checked on Amazon to find My Magical Moments Journal was uploaded and ready to be purchased.

A dream came true. Being able to say, "I did it!" felt great.

My publisher, Andrea Seydel, hosted a zoom launch party, and several family and friends attended. It was moving that people took their time to join the celebration.

A question Andrea wanted to ask me was, "What was my favourite part of the Journal?' I like quotes, of which there are about 115 in the Journal, and I like the movie Field of Dreams, so I thought my favourite part was a short dialogue from the movie that I had added.

When asked about my favourite part, this is how I answered ...

During the day of the launch party, I was out doing some errands, and when I got home, I put on the TV as I had a snack and cleaned the kitchen. Unfortunately, the TV turned on to a cooking channel which had no interest, so I changed the channel. That new channel was playing Field of

Dreams, and the timing was such that it was right at the part from where I took this dialogue.

Ray Kinsella (Kevin Costner) speaks with Archie "Moonlight" Graham (Burt Lancaster) in his doctor's office. Ray is an owner of a farm in Iowa where he built a baseball field because of a strong intuition that "if he built it, they would come," and "they" being great historical baseball players. Archie "Moonlight" Graham was a player who had played only half an inning in the "bigs."

Ray, "If you could do anything you wanted, if you could have a wish …". Archie, "And is there enough magic out there in the moonlight to make this dream come true?" Ray, "What would you say if I said yes?" Archie, "I think I'd actually believe you."

As I was telling this story, I wanted to remind people to think of the title as a metaphor and think of "field" not just as the apparent physical space but the field of energy that we can connect with: the place from which dreams come true.

When we are out of alignment with who we are or living an existence of distress and dis-ease, we can't fully access the field of dreams. We can't be fully engaged in toxic workplaces, and it's hard to be our best. When we can't answer what we genuinely want, the receptivity of the field is low. And dreams don't come true from depletion.
In June 2010, I had enough of the suffering I was experiencing privately from two stress-induced

health issues. Burnout is the most specific descriptor of how I existed. I decided there had to be a different way to do my life than that; there had to be a better way.

The Journal replicates the journey and learning from waking up that day. I had been journaling about how tired I was and how much work was a horrible grind. I decided to begin that day to write about magical moments, and that changed my life.

I am not advocating we deny the challenges we all face. However, we can choose to shift to feel better despite all that is going on. And feeling good is the only way to connect with the field of dreams.

Through the Journal and mainly through the writing about magical moments, I hope to show people a way to experience more good.

When coaching new salespeople years ago, some would ask how to "make it." I responded that they had to make enough effort to create the environment for things to happen. Of course, that wasn't scientific, but it proved it out. In addition to creating the environment for accessing the field of dreams, a foundation of well-being is essential and the only sustainable way. A few benefits of well-being include
- Reduced anxiety.
- Improved immune functioning
- Cognitive clarity.
- Better sense of self-regulation.

- Increased self-esteem.
- Reduced risk of depression.

While accessing the field of dreams might sound for some to be, well, "dreamy," there is good science behind how to access it.

May your access to the field of dreams be easy, and may you have many "home runs."

Insight Sixty-Nine:
Enduring. It's Ours to Decide

When I was a Branch Leader in the wealth management business, my favourite thing was to help Wealth Advisors make their business better: more efficient, offer more value, and be sustainable.

Some Advisors had a mindset that what had worked to get them to that point would be enough to keep it going: the future would take care of itself. But unfortunately, that was an illusion for these people: not doing things differently was, in effect, a strategy of slow decline.

I used to show advisors detailed statistics on their business. The first group didn't seem to care. The other group saw the numbers as being accurate and the result of every decision they made. Therefore, they knew that each new decision would evolve a future business: worse, the same, or better.

This group realized they had two jobs. One was to do the day-to-day business well, and the other job was to keep an eye on the future sustainability of the business to ensure each choice made the future better.

These people made conscious decisions about the plan for the future as much as for the daily goals.

285

These people knew that if they made intelligent future-based decisions each day, there would eventually be a crossover of the future business being the business they had.

I remember speaking to a very successful wealth advisor at another firm who wanted to create an enduring business. His meaning was that while he loved the industry, he wouldn't be around forever. This person valued his clients so much that he wanted to create a business that would endure beyond him.

That story is true and metaphorical in that we are all on some trajectory that is reflective of our choices, and on any given day, we could look at our "scorecard" and reflect on the stats of our own life. In our private world, each makes choices that reflect how we exist.
Collectively, all of us are making choices that reflect the evolution of our species, like a global "scorecard."

A few years ago, I heard Mary Robinson, the then Prime Minister of Ireland, speak about climate change. She was clear about the challenges facing us and emphatic that no one person should be exempt from contributing to solutions.
We, humans, tend to think linearly: tomorrow will be pretty much the same as today. Evolutionarily, we only had to worry about today and tomorrow. But technology is growing exponentially, and the

planet's resources are degrading at a faster rate than we can naturally adapt.

As little as 50 years ago, there were more fish and bigger fish. There has been a drop of two-thirds in large fish in the last 100 years. Some people think that 50 years from now, most of the fish in the oceans will be gone.

Now, you might be inclined to change the channel as I did the other day. I flipped on the TV while having my lunch and went to a series of 8 movie channels we subscribe to. One was a documentary called Sea of Life from 2016 about all threatened ecosystems. That looked heavy, so I changed to a mind-numbing alternative that I can't even remember. But before I got wholly numbed out while eating my sandwich, I consciously needed to turn back to Sea of Life.

It's six years old at this writing and is very clear and to the point: we are at risk.
Several years ago, we went to Cuba. The resort had a boat tour and snorkeling trip. We arrived at the snorkeling spot, and while we were getting ready, I spied the guide throwing bread crumbs off the other side of the boat.
Once in the water, we saw that the coral reef was mainly dead, and the bread crumbs had attracted only a few fish. That was a shocking experience. After that, my wife and I spent more time snorkeling to collect plastic bottles and garbage off the shallow seafloor than looking for more fish.

Life is fragile. A normal body temperature is about 37 Celsius, fever and illness are evident at 38 Celsius and above, and hypothermia kicks in at 35 Celsius. It's curious that the planet also has a low threshold for temperature change, or at least that we can tolerate. Scientists talk about a 2-degree Celsius increase threshold that must be avoided by 2050, or worse things will happen.

Two or three degrees are critical to life.
I wonder if we all took up a second job—a job of doing something for the future. Doing something that collectively helps our planet endure: some results we will see, and some will be for future generations to be grateful for.

The other day leading up to the Canadian election, I saw a TV ad that showed one Party's Leader followed by a list of criticisms and extrapolative conclusions about inept leadership, "therefore vote for us" was the pitch from the other Party. That was so pathetic and weak. I just thought, "really, is that best you've got? Surely to god politicians could for once think at a higher level of urgency."

The idealist in me thinks politicians should come together, grow up quickly, and work together at the highest level possible, taking up additional portfolios to fix some of the planet's most pressing issues.

288

I think we all have two jobs. Job one is living our best life, and job two is making choices to contribute to the enduring future life of the planet, the only one we can call home.
Off to do a big garbage pick-up this weekend. What inspires you to do for a better world?

Embedded in this link is a United Nations report on their 17 Sustainable Goals and a 30-minute video. The video is well worth watching. It is a sad and sobering look at the "scorecard" we have created at one level. And the video also presents inspiring and hopeful solutions for our better future together. United Nations Sustainable Development Goals and Urgent Action Video

Insight Seventy:
Smiling is a Serious Matter

On Tuesday, I led one of my weekly mindfulness coaching sessions. I started with a body scan, a progressive check-in of attention, and intentional relaxation of the feet, the legs, seat, torso, shoulders, and head. When I came to the head, I suggested the participants allow a soft smile to arise.

I smiled too, and I could feel the subtle better feeling that emerged when I smiled. Afterward, when we had a chance to reflect, one of the participants commented on how nice it was to smile and how smiling is proven to release certain chemicals that have healthy outcomes.

Smiling makes us feel good—great, real-time biofeedback.

Some research suggests

smiles evolved over 30 million years ago as monkeys and apes use a "fear grin" to signal a harmless or submissive posture. Maybe the translation of that early grin is to say, "Hey dude, no threat here. I want to hang out, be friends, and help each other. Better that way, don't you think."

Smiling is a pro-social behaviour that communicates, without spoken words, likeability, approachability, and connectedness. One of these forms of connection is in finding a partner: a smile is very attractive!

I wonder if you might try this exercise. You can do this with eyes open or closed but most ideally, be present with a sense of open awareness.

Start by being in a low energy state: no smile or, better still, a frown, and allow your body to adjust into that state. Remember what it's like to feel low, unsmiling, down, unhappy or upset. Note how that feels.

Then allow a smile to arise. Just pretend if need be. And let that smile grow and be fully expressed in your face. Now allow that smile to spread through your body and adjust into that state of a full-body smile. Note how that feels.

When we pretend to smile, when we don't feel like it, it still triggers chemicals to release certain good feelings.

"Sometimes your joy is the source of your smile, but sometimes your smile can be the source of your joy." - Thich Nhat Hanh.

It may be good news for some that a pretend smile can trigger feeling better because there has been a

291

surge in depression and anxiety over the last two years due to the global COVID pandemic.

Many people are much less happy. But, of course, there are obvious reasons and painful experiences many have gone through. I am not saying to ignore those feelings and experiences. And some people have needed professional help and medication.

Science shows that smiling is an evolutionary thriving strategy because two essential chemicals get released into our bodies when we smile. The first is dopamine, and the other is serotonin.

Dopamine is released in the hypothalamus in our brain and gives us a feeling of happiness. Conversely, low levels of dopamine cause depression, and depression weaken us in many ways, one being our immune system.

About 10% of serotonin gets released in our brain stem and 90% in our gut. Serotonin reduces stress, but low levels cause depression and aggressive tendencies.

When we smile, even if forced in front of a mirror on a tough day, the dopamine and serotonin taps get turned on instantly.

When we smile, we feel good and become happier. As a result, our immune system works better. And our heart rate and blood pressure drop to healthier levels, pain is relieved, creativity is more accessible, and a smile is contagious, all required for resilience and thriving.

When another observes our smile, they tend to feel at ease, a sense of connection, attraction, and trust, and these are critical elements of engagement at work or before walking down the aisle! Whether a leader or a lover, smiling matters.

Finally, and back to the exercise of turning a frown into a smile. When we smile, many good things turn to our favour and those we interact with like better health and better relationships.

When I led people in that body scan, and I suggested people allow a smile on their face, I could sense the fast, quiet flow of chemicals at work flushing through me, causing a sense of relief and ease.

Kids smile around 400 times a day. Those who used to be kids smile about a tenth of that.

Smile more; it's all better that way!

Insight Seventy-One:
Giving Thanks

In Canada, it is Thanksgiving weekend. Not sure what the big dinner will be, but our family will be all together for it, and that's what matters most.

Last weekend was our anniversary. We went out for dinner and got a table on a patio. The waiter gave us a menu of meals they had in the back. Somebody sourced all that food and ingredients from a few or many locations. Maybe the meat was local. Perhaps the olive oil came from the Mediterranean. I had a Trappist Ale from England. Who made the AMAZING Sticky Toffee Pudding, and thanks for the extra scoop of vanilla ice cream!

Going out for dinner was SO great! I hope I never again take for granted the pleasure and privilege of having a meal out.

My daughters are back to in-person school. I am pretty sure their enthusiasm and smiles aren't because they all of a sudden love school more. I am more confident that the way they light up when telling me about their new friends or playing basketball is because they are so grateful to be back in a social environment that they have longed for these past 18 months of the COVID pandemic.
A friend loaned me a book called Hello Darkness, My Old Friend by Sandford Greenberg. The book is

an autobiography of Greenberg's life which has been long and very successful. When he was in university with his pal Art Garfunkel, he became blind, which reads as if it happened over a couple of weeks. However, Garfunkel and another friend helped him finish his degree, and Greenberg went on to be an inventor, worked in the White House for years, wrote books, and aspired to end blindness.

One scene that struck me was Greenberg coming out of the hospital in Buffalo, now effectively blind, and staying with his family. A few weeks before, he could see, and then he couldn't. Greenberg was sitting on a couch in despair about what the rest of his life would be like. He could hear his family fussing around him, not sure what to say or how to act.

I just came back from walking my two red labs. I could see where their harnesses were, and could grab the treats and poop bags. I could navigate easily through the gate and look for traffic as we crossed the road. I could see the nasty business and get it picked up in a bag. I could see the leaves on the trees and some flowers in my neighbour's garden. Going down an alleyway, we came across some people who wanted to meet the dogs. I could see the smile on their faces as the dogs wagged their tails.

Seeing all this and having that image in my mind of Greenberg sitting on the couch and blind for the first time didn't entirely initiate joyful backflips down the alley like Jake in The Blues Brothers, but it did make me appreciate sight all the more.

How long is the list of things to be grateful for?

I love the song Amazing Grace. There is a brilliant metaphorical line, "Was blind, but now I see." Greenberg was sitting there and may have been thinking, "could see and now am blind."

The lesson for me from Greenberg's book and his life or any life is what we can do with what we have and not be defined by what we don't have.

It seems to me Greenberg came to see a possible future despite his blindness that he pursued step by step, challenge by challenge.

I read a line in a book I was reading last night called A Fistful of Wisdom that struck me. It read, "Life belongs to those who love it."

To me, that means to live in appreciation of what we have. Once in a while, maybe even to be blown away by how much we have. And sometimes, to sit for a moment and think about being able to see.

May you fully appreciate what you have, give thanks this weekend, and live daily in heightened awareness of what is most important to you.

Insight Seventy-Two:
What Should We Perpetuate More Of?

per·pet·u·ate
- to cause something to continue indefinitely.

But I could go on and on …

At the most fundamental level, all life is self-perpetuating. For us, about 1% of our cells, or 330 billion cells, die and reproduce each day, or about 700 million in the time it takes to read this Insight. And every cell in any living thing that reproduces comes standard with onboard intelligence that knows precisely what part of our life it helps perpetuate.

The life in us and all around us has been self-perpetuating and evolving for 3.5 billion years.

However, a group with a long name but essential business, the Intergovernmental Science-Policy Platform on Biodiversity and Ecosystem Services (IPBES), launched in 2019 a Global Assessment Report on Biodiversity and Ecosystem Services. Unfortunately, the short story is a bad one in that the Report reveals "that 1 million species of plants and animals are under threat of extinction." The UN-backed Report came from 15,000 scientific and government studies and was reviewed and signed off by 132 UN Member countries.

"Nature's dangerous decline is unprecedented, but it is not too late to act. Incremental change will not be sufficient – the science shows that transformative change is urgently needed to restore and protect nature." Dr. Anne Larigauderie IPBES Executive Secretary
UN-Backed Report on the human threat to nature.

I have seen headlines like, "The sea is running out of fish ... " - National Geographic But cynically, I feel when people read that they think, "Ok, wait a minute, I'll still be able to get fish for my big family gathering, a week Friday, right? Phew!"

When people say, "Oh, isn't it great that it is so warm in October!" Don't we know it's a massive problem that it is so warm in October? Today is nice and warm, but the long-term consequences are not so nice.

I am part of a group called, Don't Mess with the Don. The "Don" is the Don Valley Ravine, a 500-acre park, and ravine system in Toronto. With hundreds of volunteers, we have picked up over 175,000 pounds of trash in the last three years that has been dumped or dropped.

There is some stuff that we just can't do indefinitely.

I have an uneasy feeling in my gut as I explore the net result of what we have been perpetuating.

I wonder what explains the collective behaviour that is destroying our resources? On a micro-level, why do we find trash on the side of the road or in parks? I think it comes down to some people who can't see the connection between a choice today and the collective outcome 50 or 100 years from now.

Humans primarily think linearly. What is the big deal if I enjoy shark fin soup for lunch, hunt an elephant for sport or a tusk, overfish the oceans, or toss my empty take-out lunch bag out the window? It doesn't matter to my life, they might say.

Extinctions are long events and far away in another land. They don't happen in front of us unless it's the last one. Someone else will take care of the pollution and climate problem, I'm busy.

Society seems to perpetuate stress and ill health, which are at record levels. There is a loneliness epidemic. Teen depression, anxiety, and suicide are at record levels.

Several years ago, I went through a difficult period in my life that, in retrospect, was a great learning ground only because I learned how to shift from perpetuating one thing to perpetuating another.

My unhealthy behaviour was causing what felt like an indefinite grind. I knew I was exhausted, but I didn't change my sleep. I was irritable a lot and did nothing to change. I was burning out at work and kept doing everything that supported more of it and insanely hoping for a way out.

I used to think, 'I'll just get a good night's sleep tomorrow night, and I will feel better." Even if I honoured that cry from my body, it was just one night, incremental and not transformative.

So far, this Insight is pretty dreary, and we don't like gloomy things. We like happy endings. We want to think it will all be ok and turn out for the best. But our story only gets better if we do better individually and collectively.

In my case, I woke up one day and decided there had to be a different way to do my life than the quiet misery; there had to be a better way. The magic for me was when I realized that I was better for everyone else if I cared for myself first or equally with others.

I read a book once that talked about the idea of checking in on life at "half time," like a football game in the locker room and asking, "How is it going so far?" It seems to me at "half-time" or any other time, we are precisely at the result of every choice we have made up to that point.

Mindfulness is a natural capacity that gets strengthened by paying attention, usually to the breath: changing the brain. A few "side-effects" of practicing mindfulness is empowered awareness. This awareness naturally leads to a greater capacity to think about our thoughts. Realizing we can think about our thoughts allows us to be curious about how these thoughts serve us or not: like being an observer so we can act more thoughtfully.

We can imagine someone living an unhealthy life of poor sleep, bad diet, sedentary lifestyle, and a self-critical, limiting mindset, which is unsustainable and perpetuates unease and illness: this is not fixed; the outcome is not yet written. However, at an individual level, we can change the trajectory of our lives with effort and perpetuate something new.

Similarly, what we are collectively perpetuating for our planet is not fixed and not yet written but requires paradigm shifts of thinking and acting.

Our unconscious natural pulse that perpetuates life, cell reproduction, healing, and our immune system is one thing, a big thing, and our conscious choices about how that existence unfolds are another.

On an individual level, our best intentions should be about perpetuating happiness and wellbeing. That is the most optimal mental and physical environment from which we can express ourselves at the highest possible level. When we are happy and mentally and physically well, we thrive, which is good for everyone.

And I think when internal wellbeing shifts its trajectory in the right direction, we can more clearly see what else we can do to contribute to the external world we all share. No one deserves to be exempt from a higher degree of wellbeing, and no one should be exempt from contributing to a healthier world.

"Life is occupied in both perpetuating itself and in surpassing itself; if all it does is maintain itself, then living is only not dying." - Simone de Beauvoir.

The degradation of the resources and environment we need for survival is not sustainable. But growth is a natural state. So, we feel good in growth mode. But unfortunately, humans have compromised the healthy state of the planet and ourselves by reducing the capacity to perpetuate sustainably.

The other day I led a weekly mindfulness coaching session. With eyes closed, after leading the group in some breathing patterns and a short relaxation exercise, I suggested they imagine they had a first-class ticket on a COVID-free trip to a special destination they have been to or wish to go. In that place, I suggested they find a quiet place to sit and be with their chosen environment.

I suggested this place be restorative and safe. And their preferred location to be absent of any judgment, criticism, or need for regret or apologies, only of learning and growth. A place of unconditional positive regard for oneself. A place they could leave from and feel whole and healthy and come back to when needed.

The one thing I would have added was to imagine that the freedom from any mental obstructions they may have allows a feeling of positive, confident anticipation like being on the leading edge of possibilities for their life and all living things.

Let us perpetuate more of that.

OUR HUMAN CAPITAL

Hi my name is John,

I grew up and still live in Toronto. I'm married and have three daughters and two red labs, Juno and Chili. I swam competitively when I was young, then got into marathon swimming when I was older. I still hold the fastest time across the traditional route of Lake Ontario (51km).

I was the Chairman of the 1997 Special Olympic International World Winter Games. I have climbed Mount Kilimanjaro and Mount Kenya. I worked hard in my career in the financial business, but because I thought I was such a tough guy, I denied looking after myself for a while to try to be the best at many other things. That didn't work so well for me.

Not taking good care of me caused a few nasty health issues and burnout. The magic in my life was getting further and further away, and mostly I was experiencing a lot of stress and unhappiness. Living with anxiety and unhappiness is entirely a self-imposed state. I wanted to be happier more often and the only person who could sort it out was me, which I did, and everything got better and more manageable.

I have a business called Our Human Capital that intends to help people optimize their unique resources to do life well together through writing, coaching, and speaking. Or another way to say is I love to help people experience more great and less grind.

We all deserve to be happy, healthy, and vibrant and busting with how extraordinary life is. Right, it's not easy sometimes, and we shouldn't pretend it's all happy, happy all the time. However, we can acknowledge the difficult things, show compassion for others' suffering and ours and do our best to move from wherever we are to a little better and then a little better still. In those little or big shifts to better is the magic!

I hope these Insights have helped you to experience more great in your life!

Live Life Happy-Publishing

Helping people painlessly give birth to books that change lives.

Dear Reader,

Thank you for purchasing this unique book and joining the **Live Life Happy Community** of readers. We are a publishing company that is committed to bringing positive, supportive and well-being-enhancing books to life.

As a welcoming gift, we'd like to offer you free access to the **Live Life Happy Book Vault**, which is full of resources and support to help you live a flourishing life. You can gain access here: www.andreaseydel.com.

Finally, if you or someone you know has been thinking about writing a book, sharing a message or gaining credibility in an industry, I can help you painlessly give birth to your book. As a book doula and founder of LLH Publishing, I help make authors **booking- writing dreams *come true*.** Best of all, these books are changing lives, and your message can help others too. So don't hesitate to reach out and set up a Book Chat, and please stay in touch!

Sincerely, Andrea Seydel (The Book Doula)

Questions? Comments? Contact me at andrea.livelifehappy@gmail.com.

P.S. Books Change Lives: Whose life will you touch with yours?

Manufactured by Amazon.ca
Bolton, ON